THE CALL

Know Personally. Live Passionately

Dr. Ben Gutierrez

To Dr. Ron Hawkins,

A distinguished colleague who has encouraged me in my writing and research.

A dedicated husband and father who has been an inspiration to me to balance life, family, and ministry.

A devoted believer in Christ who has exemplified a passion for God's Word and personal holiness.

. . . and a dear friend.

Thank you.

ACKNOWLEDGMENTS

This page serves to recognize the myriad of support I received in writing this book. Without their help, I would not have been able to complete this very satisfying task.

Thank you to my wife, Tammy, whose support and encouragement through the ups and downs of life keep me going and enthused to continue to minister. I love you.

Thank you to my precious daughters, Lauren Ashton and Emma Jordan, who fill my life with such joy and laughter. I pray I live out the truths taught in this book every day before you. I love you both so much.

To Jill Walker, your acute attention to detail in managing the editing process of this book has been unparalleled. Your professionalism, knowledge of the process, and flexible spirit have been the most critical factors in finishing this book. Without your contribution, this book could not have been completed. Many thanks!

To Anne Alexander, thank you for paying attention to the smallest of details. Your technical editing improved the overall readability of the book and added the finishing touches to the manuscript. Anne can be contacted for writing and editing projects through WordWise, LLC at annea2@bellsouth.net.

To Russell Shaw, thank you for possessing such creative and artistic ability. Your work toward the illustration and design of this book has been stellar. Russell is an independent Atlanta-based designer and can be contacted by visiting russellshawblog.com.

To the leadership of Liberty University and Thomas Road Baptist Church, who provide me with the richest environments in which to edify the body of Christ. Thank you for your encouragement to write, teach, administrate, lead, and dream big. There is no better place to live, work, and minister than on Liberty Mountain!

CONTENTS

INTRODUCTION

The Questions

INTRODUCTION: *The Questions*

As a Christian, I knew the basic tenets of the Christian faith. As a pastor, I typically inserted a presentation of salvation in every sermon. But it wasn't until I became a parent that I began to feel a literal burning in my soul that moved me to articulate the truths of how someone can receive eternal salvation.

It wasn't that I lacked passion, or was careless with my presentation, or that I shared incorrect information prior to becoming a parent – not at all. But when I looked into the brilliant blue eyes of our gorgeous miracle from God, I realized that this horrible thing called "sin" would attack her little soul with zero care for how it would utterly destroy her life. It was at that moment that I felt an exorbitant sense of urgency to be able to articulate the truth that could set her free from the power of sin in this life. I also wanted to provide hope for her of forever being with the Savior of her soul. Very early on in her life, I wanted her to learn the ways of her Savior and lean on this God Who so beautifully knitted her in her mother's womb (Psalm 139:13-14).

I liken this urgency for my own child's eternal state to a familiar parental scene. You can sit in a large gym and watch 100 little neighborhood girls practice for gymnastics, but there is only one special child that consumes the parent's focus and attention. Of course, you care for the well-being of the other children. When one of them falls off the balance beam, you are concerned for their safety. But your child receives additional care and counsel from you regarding how to be safe. You caution them in the car ride to the gym. You remind them during workout breaks. And, of course, another rehearsal of all you told them on the way home from practice never hurts. These cautions are added to the multitude of daily warnings you offer your child about all the other dangerous possibilities in the world (i.e. pinching your fingers in the front door, running on the slick wood floors with just your socks on, etc.). But WHY does a parent go to this extreme to caution their child about every ill that could befall him/her? Because it's YOUR child!

This book comes out of my feeling of immediate urgency and immense care that I have for those with whom I interact and for those that I may never meet. The urgency is for everyone, regardless of age, to have a clear, concise explanation of their need for a Savior and to understand the incomparable invitation by God to enter into an intimate relationship with Him.

I am persuaded that these purposes are issues of every person's heart and a sincere seeker of truth longs to know how these principles can become a reality in his/her own life. From the moment I began my teaching and pastoring career, I have had parishioner after parishioner and student after student ask me the same questions. No matter where I was ministering, members of the body of Christ consistently approached me with the same questions.

Whether it was at the church altar after I preached a sermon, or in a hallway at the university, or in a symposium Q & A session, or through email communiqués, or in a phone call, I heard the same two questions:

"How do I know I am saved?"

"How can I grow in my intimacy with God?"

After hearing these questions time and time again, I soon found myself saying, "I need to write this down so I can simply forward the answers to anyone who asks me in the future." And finally, that day has come in the form of this book.

I pray that God will speak to you through the reading of this book and that you will be surprised by the unconditional love that the Creator of the world has for you individually. Furthermore, I pray that you will cultivate a strong desire to honor God with your life by expressing a great appreciation for Who He is and for all He has done for you.

I invite you to join me on this spiritual journey.

- Ben Gutierrez

ONE

Who You Are

CHAPTER ONE: *Who You Are*

When I was young, I remember my father asked me to go fishing with him at a state park down the highway a few miles. I loved to go fishing, so we hopped in the car and drove to the lake. We got our fishing gear out of the car, walked down the grassy hill to a semi-hidden portion of the lake, and we began to "wet a line." On that particular trip, I specifically recall catching a ton of catfish. They were biting like crazy! They were biting so well that it seemed like they were on our lines before the cast ever made it into the water. It was a great day!

When we filled the entire cooler with catfish, my father told me to make sure the cooler had fresh water for them to breathe and stay alive during our 30-minute drive home. Right then, I asked my father what to me was seemingly a very simple question to answer – "Dad, how do fish breathe under water?"

"Well, that's a good question, son," he said. And for the first time that I could recall, my father began to stumble in his explanation. Until now, in my eyes my father knew every answer to every question about everything. I remember he said, "Well, they pass water through their gills, you see?" as he pointed to one fish in the cooler. "Yeah Dad, I see, but how do they breathe air?" "Uh, well, they don't...but the water passes through their gills and there are air molecules in the water that they pick up through their gills, you see?" as he once again pointed to a different fish in the cooler. "Ok, Dad. I see their gills moving, but I thought you had to hold your breath under water because you can't breathe under water, right?"

What started as a very simple question turned into a very detailed and intricate conversation. Even though my father had a difficult time explaining the intricacies of how fish breathe under water, there was no doubt it was happening as evidenced by the catfish staring up at us watching us ponder these truths.

The same scenario seems to play out when people begin asking questions about spiritual issues – "What exactly is salvation?" "Does everyone need to be saved?" "If so, saved from what?" "How did things get this way?" What seems like simple questions are, at times, somewhat difficult to explain, even though the reality is plainly evidenced in our lives.

However, the possibility of these questions causing confusion ought not to keep people from discussing them because the answers to these questions will ultimately bring peace to the human soul.

Questions about salvation have been on peoples' hearts and minds for thousands of years. In Acts 16, we read of a jailer who was asked to detain the apostle Paul and Silas in prison for proclaiming the good news of salvation provided through Jesus Christ. Around midnight, the jailer and the other prisoners were stunned to hear Paul and Silas singing hymns of praise to God. The jailer was not accustomed to witnessing such expressions of joy, especially from two prisoners who had been publicly beaten and detained for their personal religious beliefs. This unexpected zeal must have puzzled the jailer. I wonder if he may have mentally engaged in the message of the songs that these two passionate Christian captives were singing.

As you read the story, you will note that while they were singing God miraculously liberated Paul and Silas and their fellow inmates with an earthquake. It caused all the prison doors to open and their shackles fell off. The jailer, amazed at the hand of God and grateful that the prisoners had not escaped, was led to ask a pressing spiritual question – a question that was weighing on his heart. He ran back into the prison, bowed before Paul and Silas and asked, "Sirs, what must I do to be saved?" Paul's response to the jailer is one simple statement, "Believe on the Lord Jesus Christ, and you will be saved" (Acts 16:30-31).

WHAT DOES IT MEAN TO BE SAVED?

This is a very important question – one that has both spiritual and eternal consequences. Using the Word of God, we will find the answer to this question. It is interesting that the Bible rarely provides a full teaching of every concept of a doctrine within one verse or paragraph. Rather, the Bible disperses the full teaching of a particular doctrine within a number of related verses. As a result, one will not receive a full, clear teaching of a biblical concept until all the verses related to a particular scriptural topic are researched.

This is the approach we will take in our journey through the Bible in search of a full and clear teaching of salvation. It may seem like an insurmountable task but don't be discouraged; it can and will be a life-changing journey for you. I pray you will be able to reserve some uninterrupted time to sit down to read and consider the Scriptures we will reference. They will speak profound, yet easily understandable, truths that promise to change your life forever.

Perfect clarity is needed in order to cognitively know the facts as well as the volitional requirements of salvation that result in a saving knowledge of Jesus Christ. To begin with, every Christian needs to stand firmly on the biblical truth that Jesus is the *only* way to salvation.

LET'S TAKE A LOOK

Knowing that the following verses are taken from the very Word of God, let's be patient and careful as we look at the following biblical passages. They will either confirm our already-established salvation, or they will offer guidance on how to receive eternal life and peace with God.

Romans 3:23 teaches that we are spiritually lost and in need of salvation. "For all have sinned and fall short of the glory of God."

This verse clearly teaches us that all mankind is lost. Every person needs to be saved because every person is spiritually lost. And, unlike being lost in a forest where you may find your way out, the state of spiritual lostness cannot be remedied by human means. Why? Because it is our very nature to sin.

Our souls are not lost because of the sins that we have committed. Rather, we commit sins because of our nature – our natural sinful state. Unfortunately, we often hear folks share the gospel by saying, "You must be forgiven for the bad things you have done." No. Our souls are condemned because of our sinful state, which is present in all mankind at birth. When believers share the gospel, they typically refer to the fact that the listener has sinned, but the listener must be led to understand that we commit sinful acts because we have a sinful heart and out of that sinful core, we manifest our true nature. Even though a person may not *feel* they are a sinner in need of salvation, the truth is, they are a sinner. One's need for salvation is based on this truth, and it is crucial to convey this truth to nonbelievers.

In our society, most people don't like being lumped in the same category with murderers and kidnappers. Furthermore, they see things like cheating on taxes, swearing, or telling little white lies as not so serious. But to God, sin is sin because it is a manifestation of what is at the very core of our being. If our gauge for holiness is to compare ourselves with other human beings, I am sure we could all find at least ten people who we would compare to very well. But the Bible teaches us that the true gauge is God's holiness, the perfect glory of God – a standard far beyond our ability to reach.

Romans 6:23 teaches that we deserve to be punished because we have a sinful heart. "For the wages of sin is death, but the gift of God is eternal life in Christ Jesus our Lord."

Because of our sinful state, we have earned God's holy wrath. Our culpability for our sin is likened to how we expect to receive a paycheck from an employer after we complete a job. Once we have performed our job, we expect and deserve to be paid. Another example would be a criminal who is caught for committing a crime, deserving his sentence to prison. Because of our sinful state, because we have "fallen short of His glory," all of the souls of humankind deserve to be judged by God and receive a guilty verdict from Him. And, upon receiving this verdict, the human soul is promised to be the recipient of a very tough, yet deserved, sentence . . . unless we can find Someone who is able to take upon Himself the penalty for our sinfulness and satisfy the judgment of God – releasing us from having to pay the penalty ourselves. The exciting truth is that this is indeed possible, but first you must conclude that there is no viable way you can personally pay the penalty for your own sin.

Isaiah 64:6a teaches that prior to salvation, even our best deeds or intentions are ineffective to save, and thus any attempt to save our own souls is repulsive to God. "But we are all like an unclean thing, and all our righteousnesses are like filthy rags . . . ."

Our righteousness, or good behavior, is as "filthy rags" in God's eyes. This means that every attempt to achieve salvation on our own is impossible. Every good deed, charitable action, thought, or even our sincere pursuit and intention is unclean and unacceptable. To think that we could merit salvation by our own efforts is nauseating and offensive to

> **"BUT TO GOD, SIN IS SIN BECAUSE IT IS A MANIFESTATION OF WHAT IS AT THE VERY CORE OF OUR BEING."**

the God who is the only One able to provide a sufficient payment for our sin.

Even though an unsaved person can perform charitable deeds and express kindness that reflects Christianity, at best he is performing those actions while wallowing in a sinful state – a realm that is offensive to God. Therefore, it is not the actions that save, but the change of heart behind the actions that is required.

> "THIS MEANS THAT EVERY ATTEMPT TO ACHIEVE SALVATION ON OUR OWN IS IMPOSSIBLE."

Unfortunately, sometimes people don't even know they are living a life that is offensive to God. They never realize that regardless of their culturally approved, or even church approved lifestyle, if their sinful state has never been addressed through God's forgiveness and cleansing, their actions come from a heart that is repulsive to God. For example, it would be the same as accepting the words, "I'm sorry, please forgive me" from a person who was in the middle of plotting their second attempt to steal your belongings. The words, if devoid of context, sound good, but they are not backed up by a heart that is pure and clean. Again, it is our sinful state that has earned us God's wrath and judgment and any "cleaning up" of our actions, words, or deeds without experiencing true heart change is, in effect, futile and powerless because it is done from a heart that is an offense to God.

Titus 3:5 teaches that there is no possible way to obtain salvation by our good thoughts or good deeds. "Not by works of righteousness which we have done, but according to His mercy He saved us, through the washing of regeneration and renewing of the Holy Spirit."

This verse illustrates that there is only One who provides the cleansing of our sinful state – God Himself in the form of the Holy Spirit. We have seen that we cannot save ourselves; we need God to save us. It is all about what God does in this one-sided process for us. This is further developed in Matthew 5:3, "Blessed are the poor in spirit, for theirs is the kingdom of heaven." We cannot bring anything of spiritual value in and of ourselves to the table that could positively persuade God to establish peace with Him apart from receiving His forgiveness.

When we approach the spiritual "bargaining table" with God regarding our salvation, it is actually a place where we simply plead with Him for His grace and mercy. There is no bargaining at all in this one-sided arbitration. We cannot approach God and say, "Let me remind you who my parents were," or "Here is my stellar history of community service," or "Look at all of my accomplishments." There is literally nothing that we can put on the table that can entice God to say, "Wow! Now this guy really lived a great life. If anyone deserves heaven, it should be him!" On the contrary, Matthew 5:3 teaches that if you want to enter into the Kingdom of God, you must acknowledge that you are "poor in spirit," no matter what you have accomplished in your life.

In the original language of the New Testament (called "koine Greek" pronounced "COIN-ay"), it is interesting that there were actually two words for the word "poor. The Holy Spirit could have chosen either one to describe one's spiritual state in Matthew 5:3. One of the words is the word penichros (pronounced PENny-cross) which means that someone is "needy" or "poor." This would refer to someone who has some possessions but needs additional things to add to his collection of possessions (e.g. you have a car, but need gas; you have a house, but need food, etc.). But that is not the word that is translated "poor" in Matthew 5:3.

The word used in this verse is "Ptokos" (pronounced "p-toe-COSS") which means "totally destitute" or "utterly impoverished." This word is used to describe someone who literally has absolutely nothing. This same word is used in the gospel of Luke to describe a beggar who is extending his arms asking for alms on a street corner. Being incredibly ashamed of his destitute state, he chooses to hide his face in shame as he pleads for alms (Luke 18).

Therefore, Matthew 5:3 teaches that the one who approaches God and receives salvation has nothing to offer God in his attempt to persuade God to save him. The individuals who will inherit eternal life are those who come to God recognizing and acknowledging that they have nothing to change their sinful state. They understand that, without God's intervention, they ought to be the recipients of punishment.

As a professor, I have no greater joy than to watch students grow academically, socially, physically, and spiritually. There are some students I tend to interact with more than others because they are enrolled in a particular training program. It is with these students that I have more occasion to "do life" with on a regular basis. Throughout the years, we interact formally in the classroom and informally in the office or hallway as we flesh out various issues, decisions, and challenges. Most of the time, these conversations are positive and amicable, but sometimes a conversation may be prescriptive, or involve a soft reproof due to a recent poor choice or action taken by the student. It is never easy to confront a student and talk about their poor choices, but it is all a part of demonstrating to the student that I sincerely care for their well-being, character, and testimony.

I recall a new professor who joined our university faculty who asked me about how to strike the right balance in the professor-student relationship. He inquired how to balance having a friendship with the student while at the same time reserving the right to correct the student, if necessary. I responded by describing how God deals with us as His children.

God loves us and wants the best for us. He lovingly maintains a standard of personal righteousness that is required of every person. God will not lower this standard because that would be a lie, and it would not be in the best interest for the person. Likewise, we as professors must confront only when necessary, always asking ourselves what is the best piece of advice for this student.

Then I told him that the way you know you have struck the right balance is when, at the end of their academic career, you have that bitter-sweet feeling of joy and sadness as you see them walk across the stage and celebrate the completion of one phase of their life. You know you have poured your life into them, you wish you could have done more, but you are thankful for the rich times you experienced together.

instructed the new professor on one more scenario that he might come up against when a student he knows well confesses to him and admits guilt and responsibility for a wrong doing, without making excuses or trying to hide the truth. I advised him it is at that point you want to show the student mercy and try to work with him, because in his heart he understands and accepts both the weight of his actions and the value of the mercy you will show him.

That is exactly what our Lord requires of us as we approach Him and acknowledge that we are "poor in spirit." As we recognize our guilt and our inability to rectify it, only then do we understand the true value of the mercy God lavishes upon us.

Ephesians 2:8-9 teaches that no person is able to boast about how they are able to save their own soul because salvation is made available in the form of a gift from God to all who desire to receive His salvation. "For by grace you have been saved through faith, and that not of yourselves; it is the gift of God, not of works, lest anyone should boast."

The Bible teaches that God invites anyone to accept His free gift, knowing that sufficient payment cannot be found within the power or abilities of the person who stands in need of salvation. This payment for sin does not spring forth from a heart that is tainted with sin. You cannot change your spiritual state by some deed or physical act. The best deed done with the purest of intentions in man's eyes will never be able to change his spiritual state of sinfulness.

I repeat, it is impossible to change your spiritual state by physical means. I liken it to when people get emotionally depressed. They just sit in front of the television or eat a gallon of ice cream to appease their deep-seated pain. The TV and ice cream may provide a temporary getaway from one's problems, but they certainly don't confront the root of the problem. Even Judas Iscariot, after betraying Jesus Christ and feeling a deep emotional regret, went back to the Sanhedrin and tried to return the thirty pieces of silver in an attempt to appease his condemned conscience, but his attempt was futile (Matthew 27:3-5). Regardless of how much we would want to save our own soul, we cannot change our spiritual state ourselves. Therefore,we cannot brag to others that we had any part in our salvation. It is "by grace you have been saved through faith," meaning that salvation is through trust and total dependence on God to save you. Salvation cannot be produced from within ourselves; it is a gift that only God can give you.

According to Ephesians 2:8-9, the payment for one's sin must come from a source that is holy, righteous, and absent of any sin whatsoever. It logically follows that the gift of salvation must come from the only One who is able to produce a pure gift to appease righteous and holy judgment: God Himself. Therefore, the One before whom we stand in a guilty and sinful state is the same One we plead with to be merciful to us, to forgive us, and to extend His grace and divine mercy to us.

Romans 5:8 teaches that God extended an invitation for you to enter into a peaceful relationship with Him. "But God demonstrates His own love toward us, in that while we were still sinners, Christ died for us."

Notice that this verse begins with the word "but," contrasting any notion that we can save ourselves. This verse offers hope but not before we conclude that our soul is utterly lost and guilty in God's eyes. Prior to offering hope, this verse accentuates the impossibility of saving our own souls.

By now, have you noticed that the Bible wants to drive home the state of our lostness? Why is this? Probably because the degree to which we understand the depth of our lostness determines the degree to which we will value the gift of salvation that allows us to have peace with God. By understanding what the Bible teaches about our hopelessness without Christ, we realize that our souls need a merciful God to intervene in order to provide us the gift of salvation that we are unable to provide for ourselves.

> "...THE DEGREE TO WHICH WE UNDERSTAND THE DEPTH OF OUR LOSTNESS DETERMINES THE DEGREE TO WHICH WE WILL VALUE THE GIFT OF SALVATION..."

It is indeed a scary thing to know that, aside from God's intervention, we would forever remain in our sinful state and receive eternal judgment. In 1 John 1:5 we read, "God is light and in Him is no darkness at all." As long as we have a sinful heart that has not been forgiven by God, we cannot commune with our Creator, the God of heaven and earth. We cannot have an intimate relationship with Him. We may generally be aware that there is a "higher being" that is more powerful than we are, and we may even try to talk to Him from time to time, but we really can't have a personal relationship with Him until our sinfulness is dealt with.

Romans 5:8 adds an interesting glimpse into the gracious heart of God found in the phrase, "while we were yet sinners." The Lord Jesus Christ provided a payment for our sin even when we had no idea that we were sinners. Before we came to our senses spiritually, He had His hand extended to offer salvation for our sin. This is what should cause our hearts to grieve over a world of people who mock His name. They are completely unaware of what Jesus went through for them, and they do not realize that He is offering full salvation if they would only believe in Him and receive

His free gift. It is sobering to know there are people walking around today that have physical, economical, familial, or political peace, but not peace in their soul through Jesus Christ. People's souls do not receive punishment because of a lack of an invitation to receive that peace, but because they will not accept Christ's payment for sin.

Romans 10:9-10 teaches that if we want to accept Christ, we must respond in TWO ways. "That if you confess with your mouth the Lord Jesus and believe in your heart that God has raised Him from the dead, you will be saved. For with the heart one believes to righteousness, and with the mouth confession is made to salvation."

This passage teaches us that we must respond in two ways. Responding in one way without responding in the other way does not result in salvation. Before we can confess with our mouth the Lord Jesus, we must first have a cognitive understanding of four facts:

1. Agree with God regarding our sinful state.

We must be in agreement that our sinful state merits judgment and spiritual death. We must concede that we deserve to pay the penalty for our sin.

2. Believe that Jesus is God.

We have to believe that Jesus is 100% God. If Jesus is just some man, then He is humanly unable to offer salvation. If He's just a good teacher, then He is unable to offer forgiveness of sins through His salvation. If this were true, He could only point you to a way of salvation rather than say, "I am the way, the truth, and the life. No one comes to the Father except through Me." (John 14:6).

3. Believe that Jesus' sacrifice was the only sufficient sacrifice to atone for your sin.

We must believe that Jesus' sacrifice is sufficient in totality, and it is able to provide atonement for our sin. Atonement means to cover by virtue of providing a payment. Sufficient means that the atonement was not only paid in full, but it was the only payment possible to fully pay for our sin. In other words, we don't need anything else. Jesus Christ's death on the cross and resurrection are totally adequate to atone for our sins and our sin debt.

Again, the reason why Jesus had to die on the cross was because our sin debt needed to be paid for. Someone was required to pay the price. Without Jesus, we are compelled to pay this eternal price ourselves. Prior to accepting Jesus Christ's payment for my sin, I was the one who, upon death, would have been called upon to pay for my sin. However, I applied Jesus Christ's payment to my heart and received His salvation, accepting His payment for the sin debt that I owed.

4. Believe that Jesus physically rose from the dead, thereby proving that He can conquer both physical and spiritual death.

Romans 10:9-10 says, "that if you confess with your mouth the Lord Jesus and believe in your heart that God has raised Him from the dead, you will be saved. For with the heart one believes to righteousness, and with the mouth confession is made to salvation."

In our finite human minds, we may not have a problem believing that Jesus lived or that He forgives sins, but it may seem difficult to fathom that Jesus Christ also arose from the dead. Fortunately, the truth of His resurrection is clearly taught and concretely defendable. In order to accept God's offer of salvation, we must believe fully that Jesus physically rose from the dead, and is alive and well in heaven today.

JUST KNOWING ISN'T EVERYTHING

> "FORTUNATELY, THE TRUTH OF HIS RESURRECTION IS CLEARLY TAUGHT AND CONCRETELY DEFENDABLE."

Like I said at the outset, sometimes seemingly "simple" questions are weighted with great significance and meaning – especially questions that deal with issues of spirituality, one's soul, and the need to have true peace with God. This chapter has served to provide a straightforward explanation of some spiritual questions that everyone must answer in his/her life. Fortunately, the Bible offers some clear answers to these important questions. There is more to this spiritual discussion though.

Now that we know exactly what salvation is, it is equally important to know what it is not. Salvation is not just a matter of cognitive knowledge – knowledge alone is not enough. We'll discuss this further in the next chapter.

WRITE IT DOWN:

As you read this chapter, what one Bible verse really struck you as profound or surprising? Why?

Reflect on your salvation story (if applicable) and spend some time writing about when you came to a cognitive knowledge of who Jesus Christ is and what He has done for you.

If you have not yet accepted God's free gift of salvation, spend some time writing down your questions that are still unanswered. Consider what factors are keeping you from surrendering your life to Jesus.

Write down your thoughts about what this chapter taught you about becoming a believer.

NOTES

TWO

Whose You Are

CHAPTER TWO: *Whose You Are*

This may surprise you — for sure it shocked me when I personally contemplated what I'm about to share. The more I have searched the Scriptures, I have discovered a very distinct difference between simply knowing only the facts about God and knowing those facts along with knowing the God of the facts. There is an unmistakable difference between those two scenarios.

You may have read the previous chapter's cognitive facts and got excited about these great truths, but the key question is this, "What makes true belief in Jesus Christ any different from what the demons believe about Him?" They acknowledge the exact same four cognitive facts about Jesus Christ.

In the book of James, the Bible says, "Even the demons believe — and tremble!" (James 2:19b). Further, in Mark 1:24 we see that demons believe every single fact I have listed. There was one encounter where the demons came to Jesus while they possessed an individual and one of them said, "What have we to do with You, Jesus of Nazareth? Did You come to destroy us? I know who You are —the Holy One of God!"

I would actually like to get some church members to say something like that on occasion. We know biblically that demons can never be saved because they are forever against Christ. They hate Christ and do everything possible to thwart the plan of Christ. But they believe cognitively every single fact we have listed about Jesus Christ. Demons believe that He is God, and they believe that Jesus Christ's sacrifice was indeed sufficient to save sins. They also believe He rose from the dead. In fact, it seems they probably know a whole lot more about Scripture and believe it more than some professing Christians.

So, what completes the process beyond our knowledge? What is enough? After you die and you stand before God, what will you say when He asks you, "Why should I let you into My heaven?" If your answer includes the four things we have mentioned so far in this book, God's response might likely be, "The demons believe those same facts, but they can never be saved nor be the recipient of My eternal life. Then He will ask you one more question, "So if they believe these facts and they are not saved, what is the difference between them and you?" How would you answer His question? Would you know what the difference is, and would you be able to express it to God as you stand in awe before Him?

"AFTER YOU DIE AND YOU STAND BEFORE GOD, WHAT WILL YOU SAY WHEN HE ASKS YOU, 'WHY SHOULD I LET YOU INTO MY HEAVEN?'"

THE ANSWER:
A person must know the truths of Christ cognitively and believe them volitionally!

Believing volitionally is an act of the will. It is total dependence and trust in Jesus Christ. Willingly invite God to infuse your heart, which is the center of your decision-making force, with His purpose, truth and conviction. It is not belief in a creed or a mere belief system, but it is choosing to place your total trust in the Person of Jesus Christ. It must be more than the acknowledgment that demons give to Jesus Christ. The difference is in the heart's love and commitment to have Jesus as a welcomed ruler of your soul.

This is evidenced in Romans 10:9-10 where we see that when we accept Christ we are responding in two ways. The second way is volitionally — an act of the will. When we say that we "ask Christ into our heart," what does that really mean? When the heart is referenced in Scripture it often signifies thinking, not just feeling. "For as he [a man] thinks in his heart, so is he" (Proverbs 23:7). Or "For out of the abundance of the heart the mouth speaks" (Matthew 12:34b). It's a mistake, biblically and exegetically, to say that the heart is the emotion and the mind is the intellect, because often in the Old Testament the heart is coupled with words that denote thinking.

When you speak of the heart, or when you accept Christ, it is more than a cognitive action, more than credence — it is dependence and full trust in Him. We literally ask and call on Christ to infuse our lives, our hearts and our thoughts with His will. That's why Jesus in John 10:27 says that a great evidence of salvation is this, "My sheep hear My voice, and I know them, and they follow Me." Christians will not always have full agreement on all doctrines, but I know one thing: a person's good deeds or charitable actions will not save him; however, words, deeds, trust, and attitude are all great evidences that you have accepted Christ. When you are saved, your life reflects dependence on Christ and commitment to His Word. You may not know everything as a believer, but you have that passion to grow. How do you know you believe volitionally? At the moment of requesting salvation, the heart will experience these realities:

> "WE LITERALLY ASK AND CALL ON CHRIST TO INFUSE OUR LIVES, OUR HEARTS AND OUR THOUGHTS WITH HIS WILL."

Your heart will have remorse over sin.

In Matthew 5, the Beatitudes passage, we read, "Blessed are those who mourn." After you realize that you are poor in spirit, you begin to mourn; it makes perfect, logical sense. We have remorse, not just because we are caught or enslaved by sin, but because we truly feel remorse over our sin and our sinful state. We feel ashamed of our sin and because of our lifestyle, we want to change our spiritual condition. It is through this remorse that we see our need for a perfect God.

Your heart will repent for your sin.

Repentance is more than feeling bad. Repentance is turning and running, going in the opposite direction. You are literally grieved and that grief has turned your heart to run to what is right and holy. Will we be tempted to turn around and consider our old ways? Unfortunately, yes. But there will always be some level of conviction after we sin because that behavior is contrary to our newly forgiven nature.

You will request salvation from sin.

Our prayer is this: "I don't want my sinful state anymore. I don't want to function out of a state that is offensive to You, Holy God. Would You change me and give me the power to overcome sin in my life?" We see here the difference between credence and dependence. We are not just cognitively depending on Christ, but we are surrendering volitionally to

Him as well. You cannot have one without the other.

You could say, "Sure, I'll depend on and trust in Christ. He's a great guy and might make my life better." But there is no hope in such a philosophy. We cannot give this type of message to people who are suffering in the Middle East, or in the 10/40 Window, or in sub-Saharan Africa. Their lives will not be impacted by such a message. You can't just willingly say, "I'll trust Him" without knowing what you believe or even what you are saved from.

In the last chapter, we examined where every person stands in relationship with their Creator. We discussed how one can be forgiven of their sin and have an intimate relationship with God. And even though we covered a lot of detail, it may be helpful to talk about what salvation is NOT in order to solidify our understanding of salvation.

One technique to fully understand a concept is to examine the exact opposite. In looking at the contrast, we will gain a better understanding of the original concept. By studying the opposite idea, we have a more vivid understanding of what a particular verse is saying, so let's consider what true salvation is by examining what salvation is not.

> "ONE TECHNIQUE TO FULLY UNDERSTAND A CONCEPT IS TO EXAMINE THE EXACT OPPOSITE."

WHAT SALVATION IS NOT...

1. The physical act of uttering words in prayer form

In Hebrews 4:2 the author explains that the Word of God had no effect because it was not coupled with faith. Isn't that a sobering statement? The fact that the truth of God landed on ears, but it had no effect because it wasn't coupled with the heart of faith is a solemn thought, indeed. If you show a man a cue card and he spouts off, "I admit that I'm a sinner. I believe in my heart. I commit and accept Jesus Christ," I cannot automatically say to him, "You're saved!" Just getting someone to utter certain words is not evidence of salvation. The prayer of salvation must come from a heart that understands lostness, or as my friend Alvin Reid says, "their emptiness."

They must truly understand they are lost before they can know the value of being saved.

You should be very cautious and patient when getting someone to utter a prayer of salvation because their heart must already know it and believe it. I am sad to say that I can recall a time in my high school days when my goal was to get someone to say "the prayer." I went to New York City as part of an evangelistic outreach, and I had been hearing about people who had great experiences leading people to Christ. I desired to have a great evangelism story too. So I determined in my heart that I would lead a person to the Lord that day. I remember sitting on a park bench when a gentleman approached. I can even picture his face. I remember trying to rush him to say "the prayer," and I remember telling him, "Just pray this and mean it in your heart." When I'd start to pray it, he'd interrupt me and say, "But you know, I don't know." Then I quickly answered, "Just say this prayer." I remember he finally got through the whole prayer, but I thought to myself, "I feel so bad because I just led him into the act of simply uttering words."

He walked away; I never saw him again and probably never will. I pray to God that He grips that man's heart and doesn't allow that scenario to skew his thinking about the gospel. You see, salvation is so much more than words. In fact, if an individual hears and recognizes the truth of the gospel and the state of their lostness, you can then explain to them how they can have an intimate relationship with God. You can explain the truth of Jesus Christ and how He is the God who came to earth, died for us and defeated death through His resurrection. You can share how the person needs to believe these cognitive facts, but also that person needs to volitionally trust Christ.

I believe the prayer is more of a confirmation or an affirmation for the mature believer to listen in to see if the one you are sharing the gospel with understands what they just did. Frankly, they could be saved before they ever utter that prayer. It's the heart that trusts. The mind cognitively knows, but it's the heart that trusts in the Savior. In Romans 10:9-10 we read, "If you confess with your mouth the Lord Jesus and believe in your heart that God has raised

"THE MIND COGNITIVELY KNOWS, BUT IT'S THE HEART THAT TRUSTS IN THE SAVIOR."

Him from the dead then you will be saved." In the Jewish tradition, you could not say you were a believer without coupling it with action. It was absolutely, unequivocally, positively impossible to say "I'm a believer" and not live it in the 1st century Jewish custom. In Acts, when Paul says, "Repent and be baptized," we see that repentance is what literally brings salvation. The words expressing our faith in Christ are simply a confirmation of what has occurred inside us.

2. The physical act of walking down a church aisle during an invitation

Again, when people believe on Jesus Christ in their hearts during a church service, they are saved before they ever walk down the aisle. And maybe the prayer at the altar is a confirmation to believers who prayerfully watch as people come to Christ. As long as people cognitively believe and their hearts are stirred to salvation, they are probably saved prior to that physical act of walking down the aisle.

3. Contingent on a great emotion (or the lack of) during the conversion experience

Some individuals, when they're leading a person to Christ, will gauge the success or effectiveness of this endeavor on the emotional reaction of that individual. This is not a good gauge at all. Emotion is based on personality and is no indication of spirituality or of whether or not salvation "took." Some cry and some laugh. I remember leading a man to the altar, explaining the truths of Christ, and praying with him as he received salvation. After praying at the altar he stood up, shook my hand and simply said, "That was the right thing to do. That was good that I did that." No tears. No emotion.

Conversely, some people who accept Christ bawl a river of tears and get very emotional, raising their hands and dancing all around. The way in which emotions are expressed will be reflected in the individuals' personalities. The Spirit may work mightily, but if the room is filled with introverts, they will be very introspective when they get moved by the truths of the songs and Scripture. You cannot gauge even your own worship on emotion and outward expression; it must be the heart stirring, and it may not always be an overt expression.

4. The result of solely wanting to be saved from going to hell upon death

"Do you want to go to heaven or hell?" I am always curious if the person who asks this question expects to receive a different answer than "heaven." It seems to me this question may skew an unbeliever's answer and ignore the full teaching of salvation that we have been discussing in this chapter. Who would not choose heaven over hell? As a parent, I can't help but liken it to the question some parents often ask their child, "Do you want a spanking?" Think about what the child is going to say. Have you ever heard this response? "Yes! Actually, I'd like a double dose!"

Here's the problem, people don't understand the value of salvation until they understand their lostness. As we've discussed, because we are born in a sinful state, we have merited or earned condemnation to hell. It's not God being mean to us; it's our natural state. Because of Adam and Eve's choice, we've done it to ourselves. When a student of mine fails a course, I will say, "I did not fail you. You failed yourself by what you did or didn't do, and you are reaping the consequences of your actions."

Likewise, because of mankind's sin nature – because I'm not perfect like God, and I'm not as holy as He is – there is no way I am worthy of heaven without God in me. I'm not holy and my sinful heart is repulsive to God and condemns me. I deserve eternal punishment for my sinful state. Therefore, I (and all sinners) need a change of heart—one that is life-changing and soul-changing. Every human being needs salvation through Christ.

The topic of hell should never be avoided because it is the inevitable outcome for those who do not accept Christ after they have been presented with the following truths:

- *They are not at peace with God.*
- *They are in close relationship with God's wrath (Ephesians 2:3).*
- *They do not accept Christ's payment as the only way to*

appease the Father's wrath.

But hear me, I personally am of the conviction that if I turn to someone and ask, "Do you want to go to heaven or hell," they may not at that point fully understand their emptiness, or the fact that they are an enemy of God.

So I suggest that hell should definitely be part of the salvation equation, but we need to be aware that people who pray for salvation may not be thinking at the time, "I am not going to be punished eternally." The reason we are not saved is because we are not at peace with the Holy God, our Creator. As I said earlier, our Creator is the Holy One, and we must commit our lives to Him and ask forgiveness for how we have separated ourselves from Him and created the gulf between us through our sin. And hell is a byproduct of the repercussion for not believing.

5. Translated into instant perfection

As stated in the previous chapter, the Bible disperses the full teaching of a particular doctrine within a number of related verses. But there are three terms that can summarize the different aspects of the salvation process.

Occasionally when the Scriptures use the word saved or salvation, it is actually used in a few different ways. It is used sometimes amorally – like you're saved from a ship sinking or you're saved from a crowd wanting to stone an individual. Literally, salvation is used in the sense of just protection. The word salvation was not a spiritual term that biblical writers made up; it was a very practical term that was adopted to explain the saving of our souls. Hence, the word saved has taken on this real spiritual meaning and it has great depth. So when we read Scripture sometimes and it uses the word *saved*, it means the point in which you were justified, sanctified, or glorified. Let me explain.

JUSTIFICATION –
Saved from the penalty of sin

The moment an individual is saved from the penalty of sin, we literally move from darkness to light, change course from hell to heaven, and gain peace with God. Sometimes the Bible uses the words *saved* or *salvation* to refer to the moment Christ redeems us. At the moment of salvation, the individual is sealed by the Holy Spirit and becomes a child of God – a Christian. This is called justification. In fact, Paul uses this word in Romans to describe that moment – it is a judicial act or a declaration wherein God proclaims, "You are justified!" It's as if a judge slams down the gavel and authoritatively states, "Done deal!"

SANCTIFICATION –
Saved from the power of sin

Sometimes in Scripture, the word *saved* is referring to our developmental growth, spiritual growth, or maturity. Philippians 2 says, "Work out your own salvation." This is not referring to the justification aspect of salvation because you can't work out your own salvation. But you can work for, develop, and be in process of your spiritual maturity. And that's exactly what one of the terms for salvation refers to – sanctification. Once we are saved, we are to utilize the power of the Holy Spirit against the power of sin. The more you are sanctified, the more you are maturing, the more power you have against sinning because of the power source of the Holy Spirit within you. You have a mind that has been inculcated by His truths. You are to be constantly storing away and hiding God's Word in your heart. It is a lamp for your feet and a light for your path (Psalm 119:105). As you mature, you have the ability by God's power alone to say, "I'm not going to go down those old paths of sin again."

Before our salvation, according to Ephesians 2:1-3, we could not say "no" to sin. We could say, "I don't like doing these things," but we had no power to overcome the grip of sin. We, as sinners, were encased by sin. There was no way to jump out of that realm into the realm of the Holy Spirit. Now that we're in the saved realm, the Holy Spirit allows us to confidently state, "I don't want to do that action." We've been saved from the penalty of sin, and we gain an immediate power source that is our strength to overcoming the sins that once plagued our lives. We can be controlled by the Spirit (Ephesians 5:18) and therefore do not have to give in to the desires of our flesh.

GLORIFICATION –
Saved from the presence of sin

Sometimes the word salvation will refer to the consummation of our salvation. In fact, Scripture writers will use the word saved to refer to our future salvation. The fact that the "helmet of salvation" (Ephesians 6:10-17) is looking at the future aspect of salvation means that one day we, as Christians, will be saved from this world and from this environment of sin. As Christians, our salvation is settled – a done deal. But one day we will be saved from the presence of sin when we see God face to face. There will be no more warring of the soul (Romans 7), and sin won't even be a variable in our lives. That's a beautiful place – to think that someday we won't have this battle within us! We will be in the presence of the Holy One for all eternity.

Recently, I was lecturing on the benefits of heaven. I noted that we will be able to think, remember, worship, learn, work, and enjoy it all. You and I will be on the other side and we'll say, "Hey let's go worship the Holy One for a millennia or two!" And we'll just zip into His presence. There will be no sun because the glory of God illuminates the sky. We'll also recognize people and be able to talk to them, and we'll know who our loved ones are by name. What a beautiful hope we have as believers!

Titus 2:11-13 tells us, "For the grace of God that brings salvation has appeared to all men (justification), teaching us that, denying ungodliness and worldly lusts, we should live soberly, righteously, and godly in the present age (sanctification), looking for the blessed hope and glorious appearing of our great God and Savior Jesus Christ" (glorification). All three of these salvific terms are found in that one passage. These terms are important to know because we evangelize to bring someone to God in order to be justified. We see that there is an accountability, or a discipleship process, that we must be involved in all the way through sanctification to glorification – it never ends. Salvation is a glorious promise and a wonderful gift of God.

AM I SAVED?

Now that we have taken some time to learn about what salvation is and what salvation is not, I want you to ask yourself the most important question that you will ever be asked. Ask yourself, "Am I saved?"

"ASK YOURSELF, "AM I SAVED?""

We have covered a lot of ground in terms of the salvation experience and our desperate need for God because of our sin. But I want to ask you now if you are indeed a child of God. You may have been in church for a long time and heard many of these principles articulated in the pulpit. But as I've noted, salvation is more than simply hearing the message. If you examine your life, can you remember a time that you knelt before God and said, "I am a sinner and I need You to save me." Maybe there has never been a time that you processed these things and cognitively looked at what you needed to know and believe in your heart to be saved. You didn't quite comprehend your lostness, so you haven't committed your heart and trusted Christ solely for salvation. I don't know where you are spiritually. Maybe you've lived in a Christian home and have possibly lived off your parents' belief. There's never been a time where you have processed these things until now, so please ask yourself, "Do I acknowledge this? Do I cognitively know this? Do I believe this in my heart? Have I volitionally, of my own will, committed and trusted in Jesus alone? Am I totally dependent on Him?"

Be cautioned. You can be right in the middle of the church house and be lost! You can be like Judas Iscariot who walked with Jesus for over three years, but he was lost. You can be like the apostle Paul who, prior to his salvation experience, knew the Scripture writings but was looking at it through carnal eyes – as a works-based faith. He was essentially saying, "What can I *do* to get saved?" When he actually got saved, he was able to immediately become a strong minister because he knew all the truth from before, but now he was able to look at that same truth through spiritual eyes – Christ's eyes. You may know the Scriptures and all the spiritual words that so many Christians utter, but you may have learned after reading this chapter that you need to look at it differently now.

The question is this: If right now, you are not sure that you're saved (as defined in this chapter, based on God's Holy Word), would you like to take care of it now – in this moment? Would you bow your head and get in whatever posture that would cause you to focus on God and ask Him to forgive you and save you today?

WHAT MUST I DO?

In your heart you must (1) believe that Jesus is God; that He visited this earth and lived a sinless and pure life, died on the cross to make payment for your sin, arose from the tomb and invites everyone to believe in Him; (2) believe that He arose the third day to give unequivocal proof that He is sufficient to conquer death, and He will conquer the spiritual death in our lives; (3) believe your soul will be eternally His if you know those facts and couple it with a heart of faith and put your dependence and trust in Him; and (4) commit these things to Him by saying, "I believe You, and I will entrust my whole life to You based on this truth. My foundation will now be grounded on the truths of Jesus Christ, the Holy One of God."

Finally, in your own way, ask Jesus to be your Savior. And then, simply just thank Him for saving you, and thank Him that He has opened your eyes to your need of salvation.

If you have done this, God has washed and cleansed you, and your soul is as white as snow! God will give you a power source to say no to your temptations and to live for Him. You are beginning today as a Christian, as a child of God!

If you accepted Christ just now, I pray that you will inform someone of your decision, or contact me directly at Liberty University. I would love to rejoice with you. I pray that you will get involved in a church that teaches these principles from God's Word.

WRITE IT DOWN:

In the explanation of salvation, do any of the points not apply to your life? Did any one point personally surprise you, or cause you to think about what salvation is not? If so, write down your thoughts.

Take some time to think about your salvation experience (if applicable). How do you know for certain that you are saved? If you are not, what has this chapter caused your mind and heart to ponder?

NOTES

THREE

Do Justly

CHAPTER THREE: *Do Justly*

If there is one thing I have learned regarding leadership, it is that people desire clarity from their leaders. It is difficult to follow someone when their instructions are not clear. Frustration quickly sets in and you want to blurt out: "Just spit it out!" "Tell me plainly!" "Be clear!" "Tell me *exactly* what you want me to do!" I have expressed these emotions, and I am fairly certain there have been circumstances where most of us have felt the need for more clarity from the one who is in charge. But have you ever entertained these thoughts as you have studied the Bible?

Have you ever been reading the Bible and/or praying and respectfully said, "God, please tell me exactly what I should do?" Or, "Lord, please show me precisely how I should live my life today to honor you?" Or, "Jesus, what are You doing in my life? What should I be learning from these circumstances right now?" I think

> "IT IS DIFFICULT TO FOLLOW SOMEONE WHEN THEIR INSTRUCTIONS ARE NOT CLEAR."

if we are completely honest, we would have to admit that each and every one of us has asked God for clarification about how to walk as authentic Christians in this world.

I'VE BEEN THERE

I remember a time during my college years when I asked God to teach me what it truly means to "glorify Him." I had always heard that phrase in the context of people praying at church. ". . . Lord, I pray we will glorify You today." I remember thinking, "Ok, but how exactly should I make that happen in my life? What do I need to do in order to know that I am 'glorifying God' in my life?" For a number of months those questions swirled around in my mind. I prayed for an answer, but I did not receive one that appeased my curious mind. I was about to question if God had even received my prayer request.

Then one day, I was sitting in a New Testament survey class and the answer came to me. It is what God desires of every Christian and it's only one word—"Obey." At that moment, it struck me that God receives the most glory when I obey Him—plain and simple. All that time I was looking for a massively detailed explanation, a formula, or a testimonial to follow that spelled out exactly what deeds and activities I needed to do in order to bring glory to God. Ultimately, I learned that what brings glory to God is to obey His spiritual principles, and He will guide me through all of the messy circumstances of life. God specifically calls for obedience in the lives of every believer, and fortunately He never leaves us without clear principles to follow. Throughout the Old and New Testaments God has provided specific directives to guide us in our daily lives.

In these next few chapters, we will examine some extremely clear principles that each Christian should embrace as an unmistakable way to bring glory to God. These spiritual principles are easily understood, but they are challenging to live by unless your heart is in love with the God Who spoke these words. I encourage you to take a moment and reflect on the previous chapters of this book that described the gracious gift of salvation that God offers to you. In order to bolster your appreciation for the Lord and His love for you, revisit the details of Jesus' sacrifice of His own life. He paid for your sin and my sin— sins that neither you nor I could pay for ourselves. Rethink what your life would be like today if you had not accepted His gift of salvation. Recall those times of pain, loss, discouragement, and fear that you were able to endure because of your secure position in Christ. I trust that after you take some time to rehearse how God's grace has been active in your life, your heart will be ready to receive these guiding spiritual principles. As you embrace them in your day-to-day circumstances, you will bring God His deserved glory.

WRAPPED UP IN ONE

Consider these guiding principles found in one Bible verse:

Micah 6:8
He has shown you, O man, what is good; and what does the LORD require of you but to do justly, to love mercy, and to walk humbly with your God?

This verse specifically tells us how we should walk as believers in Christ in this world. The instructions are plain, simple and crystal clear. Every believer in Christ is to:

1. ***Do Justly***
2. Love Mercy
3. Walk Humbly

These three guiding spiritual principles can be understood by the youngest of believers in Christ. Yet, they should serve as a filter for all believers as we navigate through our spiritual questions in the days, months, and years to come.

NOT OPTIONAL

It would seem like no discerning Christian would avoid the instructions given to us by the Lord in Micah 6:8, but one important detail should be noted: the Lord does not give any believer an option to "take or leave" these instructions. Notice the phrase "the LORD require[s] of you." The word "require" denotes a command or demand. The Lord actually *requires* each and every believer to live according to these three directives. In this simple observation we have exposed three spiritual conditions that are not optional for a believer. Micah uses straightforward and repetitive language that reinforces the fact that there definitely is no "opt out" clause in this verse.

IT'S ALL GOOD

And why wouldn't God give us an option to pick-and-choose which directives to obey? The answer is found in the previous phrase in Micah 6:8. "He has shown you...what is good." The word "good" implies that these requirements are "valuable," "necessary," "appropriate" for all believers. The Lord prefaces what He is about to say with the fact that what He's going to require of us is both clear, valuable, necessary, and incumbent upon ever believer. Therefore, the wise believer should receive gladly the commandment of the Lord and see the immense value of obeying these commands. This combination of command and perceived value can also be seen in Psalm 15:5b where God provides a number of characteristics of true believers and also relates the intrinsic value and benefit of obeying His commands by saying, "He who does these things shall never be moved." And just as God commands and inspires His believers in Psalm 15:5, He likewise commands and motivates believers to obey—not just because they were *told* to obey, but also they need to see the value of obeying Him.

Do Justly

The first spiritual principle that should filter every decision, thought, word, and deed in our lives is taken from the phrase in Micah 6:8, "He has shown you, O man, what is good; and what does the LORD require of you but to do justly . . . ?"

The phrase "Do Justly" means to live right in the eyes of God and man. This is more than simply teaching that we ought to live a holy life before God—which is the most important thing in a believer's life. But we also are to "Do Justly" in the eyes of man, to practically exhibit our commitment to trust God's Word, God's ways and God's timing to all who observe our countenance. But what is faith if it is never put to the test?

Psalm 46 describes utter catastrophe, ruin, cataclysmic events and colossal destruction. It takes the believer back to the basics— "Don't worry, God's in control!" So, when things get ugly, we are told to remember that God is still in control.

"BUT WHAT IS FAITH IF IT IS NEVER PUT TO THE TEST?"

ENTERING A "SPIRITUAL SIMULATOR"

In Psalm 46 God is putting each believer into a "Spiritual Simulator" to see how seriously we take His command to trust Him—no matter what. Psalm 46 asks us if we would still trust God in the midst of more than minor disturbances and setbacks in our lives. It asks us to answer if we would still trust God even if major, painful life losses occurred or if the dissolution of the world and life as we know it was on the cusp of unhinging. In putting us to the test, this Psalm describes every reference to stability in ancient times and pretends for a moment that all became unstable and unhinged at their core. This Psalm asks us to react to a catastrophic scenario—"What if everything that you took as secure, predictable, stable, and foundational as laws of creation immediately and utterly got turned upside down? And while in this chaotic scenario, what if all of the people dwelling in that creation turned utterly violent? Would you still trust God?"

"Do Justly" (i.e. living right before God and man) begins by trusting God's Word. His Word is His promise. God says that He never makes a promise that will not be fulfilled. "So shall My word be that goes forth from My mouth; It shall not return to Me void, But it shall accomplish what I please, And it shall prosper in the thing for which I sent it" (Isaiah 55:11). Likewise, Psalm 46 screams at us to trust God and His promise that He is in control. You can go to the bank on the fact that God will take care of you no matter what life circumstance you are facing.

GOD IS IN CONTROL

At the very beginning of this Psalm, God reminds us that He is trustworthy. He is more than able to be trusted in any and all circumstances. Notice what this Psalm says:

Psalm 46:1-2a
God is our refuge and strength,
A very present help in trouble.
Therefore we will not fear. . . .

God is our refuge (i.e. a tower/shelter for protection), our strength (i.e. source of power cf. Eph.6:10), and our very present help in trouble (cf. a source that is always present and available). No wonder the author of Psalm 46 declares that he will not fear. But that is a very easy proclamation to declare *prior* to the experience. Anyone can claim that they will not fear prior to being tested. So, the Psalmist says, "Ok, prove it." Then he puts the reader through a spiritual simulator and causes us to react to some of the most cataclysmic, colossal, life-altering scenarios to see if our faith in God would remain strong.

God Is in Control...
WHEN OUR FOUNDATION IS SHAKEN

The Psalmist asks us to put our faith to the test to see if we will still trust God and remain strong by first causing us to imagine if everything that we considered "foundational" in our life became unstable.

Psalm 46:2-3
Therefore we will not fear,
Even though the earth be removed,
And though the mountains be carried into the midst of the sea;
Though its waters roar and be troubled,
Though the mountains shake with its swelling. Selah

This scenario would be frightening not only for believers in the ancient world, but also for believers today. Who wouldn't feel frightened over earthquakes, earth shifting catastrophes, vicious storms over the waters and volcanoes? When these cataclysmic events occur today, we all feel very helpless and powerless to control them.

Some time ago, a 5.8 magnitude earthquake occurred approx. 38 miles northwest of Richmond, VA (nearly two hours away from Liberty University, Lynchburg, VA.). I vividly remember feeling the rumbling of the earthquake as I was standing in line at the campus bookstore, waiting to order a cup of coffee. Since it was my first time to experience an earthquake, it took me quite a while to figure out what was happening. As the rumbling was building stronger and stronger, I initially thought that someone was rolling a huge, heavy cart of some kind nearby that was causing the rumbling on the floor. But as I turned around, there was no cart to be found. Then I looked behind the counter and noticed that every picture frame began to swing back and forth. It was at that moment I immediately felt a feeling that I had not felt in a long time—a sense of helplessness. This problem was much, much bigger than anything I could control. I began to ask myself, "Should I go outside away from the building?" But even then I surmised, "I still won't be able to get away from the earthquake if I go outside." Then, instantly I began to think of my family. "Where's my wife right now?" "Are my kids feeling scared right now?" "Are the leaders at their school taking good care of the children?" Needless to say, even though I tried to keep a calm demeanor on the outside, I was not so calm on the inside.

But something calmed me down completely and almost instantly right in the middle of the earthquake. I was able to experience an amazing peace as I stood in line *while* the earthquake was still vibrating the building. My spirit was calmed when I looked at the student in front of me who was standing there so calmly. He was not disturbed at all. I noticed that all throughout the earthquake, he remained so tranquil. And when the earthquake was at its peak, he simply turned to me and said, "Don't worry, it's just an earthquake . . . I'm from California . . . we see this all the time . . . it's nothing." Then I'll never forget as he turned to the barista and placed his order as if absolutely nothing out of the ordinary was going on (I believe he ordered a tall chocolate mocha, double shot, stirred – not shaken!).

I was amazed by his level of confidence in this situation, and I instantly fed off of his calm demeanor. He was tranquil in the midst of what was scaring most everyone else in the line. But he knew that all would be well and that he was not in harm's way. It helped me to see someone who was calm in the chaos. The same is with our spiritual lives. It helps to be able to witness someone who has been through what we are experiencing and see or hear them testify of God's protection. But the goal is to be that type of person that others

"BUT THE GOAL IS TO BE THAT TYPE OF PERSON THAT OTHERS CAN FEED OFF OF YOUR STRONG FAITH."

can feed off of your strong faith. And when you experience challenges that seem to shake the very foundation of your life, you still remain faithful and continue to trust in the God Who is in control.

God Is in Control...
WHEN PEOPLE COME AGAINST US

Even though foundation-shaking events impact our lives profoundly when they occur, they don't occur as often as another impactful challenge.

The Psalmist puts us through one of the most frequent challenges that affect each of us seemingly every day—people who cause us pain.

Psalm 46:4-7

There is a river whose streams shall make glad the city of God,
*   The holy place of the tabernacle of the Most High.*
God is in the midst of her, she shall not be moved;
*   God shall help her, just at the break of dawn.*
The nations raged, the kingdoms were moved;
*   He uttered His voice, the earth melted.*
The LORD of hosts is with us;
*   The God of Jacob is our refuge. Selah*

This Psalm asks if we would trust God even when the nations rage. You see, when our problems become bigger than life, we often run to God for help because it is so obvious that we cannot control the circumstances ourselves. But why is it when people begin to persecute us with their words and actions, we often doubt the power of God and His ability to get us through?

To many, the persecution from people is the most life-consuming challenge, and it causes us to doubt God's power the most. Maybe it is because we feel that colossal circumstances can be bypassed or out-smarted, but when people are in play, we believe that in some way they are able to outsmart God, His rules, and His ways. I will admit, it is tough to live with people who come against us. Our minds replay their words all day long. We think about their words as we put our heads on our pillow, and the thoughts are still with us in the morning. But make no mistake, the same God who spoke the world into being and who is able to calm any chaos in His creation can (and will) silence the actions of any person that comes against one of His believing children. Our part is to trust that God's timing is always perfect and that He will certainly deliver us at just the right time (i.e. "and at daybreak" cf. Exodus 14:27 HCSB).

How do we build our faith in Him to this level? We remember that He is a God Who is able to control people at His will the same way He is the Lord over all of the supernatural beings (c.f. "The Lord of host"). Also, we need to remember that in God it is as if we are sitting in a secure, fortified fortress (cf. "refuge" v.7, 11) protected from the sting of any attackers. Thus, we don't have to empower the words of our attackers, but rather focus on God's gracious encouragements concerning you and me (c.f. Jeremiah 29:11, "For I know the thoughts that I think toward you, says the LORD, thoughts of peace and not of evil, to give you a future and a hope.").

God Is in Control...
WHEN OUR LIVES BECOME CHAOTIC

What God does in our lives per each situation is a mere sampling of what He will one day do in total. He will ultimately deal with all the evil, but He requires us to go through these trials with His help until that faithful day.

> ### *Psalm 46:8-11*
> *Come, behold the works of the LORD,*
> *Who has made desolations in the earth.*
> *He makes wars cease to the end of the earth;*
> *He breaks the bow and cuts the spear in two;*
> *He burns the chariot in the fire.*

When things in our life become chaotic we are told to "behold" (i.e. take note of with intense interest) how God has and will ultimately deal with all the sin and chaos in our lives and in the world. In this spiritual simulator, we are encouraged to focus on God's promises and look forward to the reality that one day He will s make all of this chaos "cease" (i.e. "rest").

God Is in Control...
WITNESSING HIS POWER

At this point the simulator allows all of the chaos to swirl around us, our fears to be at their climax, and our questions to multiply . . . and then it's time to see God-in-action. God speaks with all authority to the chaos and commands it to stand down from its menacing attack against believers.

Psalm 46:10-11
Be still, and know that I am God;
> *I will be exalted among the nations,*
> *I will be exalted in the earth!*
The LORD of hosts is with us;
> *The God of Jacob is our refuge. Selah*

"Be still and know that I am God" is a strong command by God to the chaos. God commands the chaos to "Be still" (cf. cease your striving activity), "know that I am God" (cf. recognize His authority), and testify to the fact that He and He alone will be the One Who will ultimately reign in any and all circumstances of life. And our peace comes when we simply stand there and witness God-in-action as He controls all of our life circumstances.

In the middle of the madness, chaos and anxiety, we must trust that the LORD can and will step right into the middle of it and yell at the chaos, "Be still!" The God of heaven and earth will calm the raging sea of trouble, doubt, fear, and anxiety in our lives . . . but we must trust Him *prior to* experiencing His promised delivery.

> **"IN THE MIDDLE OF THE MADNESS, CHAOS AND ANXIETY, WE MUST TRUST THAT THE LORD CAN AND WILL STEP RIGHT INTO THE MIDDLE OF IT AND YELL AT THE CHAOS, 'BE STILL!'"**

WILL YOU TRUST GOD?

So, how did you do going through the spiritual simulator presented in Psalm 46? When you imagined all of these life-altering circumstances happening to you, could you see yourself trusting God in the midst of it all? Did you pass the test? Sure, we can reset the simulator even if we didn't pass the test, but in real life it is not that simple.

The first and most important way to begin to "Do Justly" is to trust the Lord in each and every circumstance of life. And one of the most necessary spiritual disciplines that a believer can cultivate is the commitment to trust God and remain faithful to Him prior to experiencing the deliverance of God. While we know that God will calm the raging sea of trouble, doubt, fear, and anxiety in our lives, we must practice trusting Him in the smaller, daily challenges of life so we are prepared prior to experiencing His promised delivery in those catastrophic events.

In addition, if the Bible is crystal clear on how we should live, then why don't we obey what the Bible teaches us? I believe the reason is simply because we choose not to obey. What is your default reaction when it comes to obeying God in your circumstances? Are you committed to obeying Him—no matter what? And most importantly, are you living out your faith in society? Consider asking a close believing friend to join you in an intentional spiritual discussion about where you are in your spiritual life. Develop a spiritual plan to practice righteousness on a daily basis, and join together in continual prayer to improve the spiritual discipline of obedience.

> **"IN ADDITION, IF THE BIBLE IS CRYSTAL CLEAR ON HOW WE SHOULD LIVE, THEN WHY DON'T WE OBEY WHAT THE BIBLE TEACHES US?"**

So the question for you and me is simple, "Will you trust God before you experience His deliverance from your challenging circumstances?" How strong is your faith at this point in your spiritual walk? What have you done to strengthen your spiritual walk? Have you taken time to talk with another believer and ask for spiritual accountability from him/her? Have you consciously inserted spiritual practices into your life that promote spirituality? Or, have you simply asked God to help you become a stronger more passionate Christian without taking any proactive steps to create positive spiritual growth in your life?

I encourage you to become proactive in doing whatever it takes in your life to build a faith in God that trusts Him prior to Him displaying His power over your circumstances. Trusting God in those times of waiting is probably the most obvious sign of a believer who truly wants to "Do Justly."

WRITE IT DOWN:

Do you really believe that God will carry you through whatever? What will it take to build your faith to the point that you will trust God prior to any challenging circumstances? Commit to spend time in God's Word each day and you will strengthen your faith muscle!

When it's obvious we can't control the circumstances we are facing, most of us immediately run to God for help, knowing He's the only One who can "fix it." But why is it that we don't take our relational issues to Him? When you are hurt by people's critical words or insensitive actions, do you trust the Lord with your attitude in those situations?

NOTES

FOUR

Love Mercy

CHAPTER FOUR: *Love Mercy*

One of the most beautiful words in the human language that brings comfort, peace, and rest to our hearts is the word, "mercy." It seems that everyone wants a merciful person near them— in marriage, in ministry, and in close friendships. A person that is full of mercy allows us to be human and to make mistakes. In their mercy they give us a second chance to live a life according to God's ways. The character trait of mercy is listed as the second spiritual discipline in Micah 6:8. We bring glory to God as we cultivate mercy in our day to day relationships.

> **Micah 6:8**
> *He has shown you, O man, what is good; and what does the LORD require of you but to do justly, <u>to love mercy</u>, and to walk humbly with your God?*

Along with the requirement to "Do Justly," the directive to **"Love Mercy"** can undoubtedly be understood by the youngest of believers in Christ. The character trait of mercy is the second filter that all believers should practice as we serve one another in the body of Christ. As we learned in chapter three, the word *require* in this verse indicates that all believers are to show mercy—it's a requirement of the Lord, not an option.

And we must once again note the preceding qualifier phrase, "He has shown you . . . what is good"—to "Love Mercy" is a valuable, necessary and appropriate conduct for all believers. Therefore, the wise believer should gladly receive the commandment of the Lord to live a life that is characterized by showing mercy.

A STORY OF MERCY

There once was a rich, wealthy King who was known for being kind and loving to all of the people in His kingdom. But most of the people thought the king was nothing more than a naïve leader because they had heard that he told a person that owed him almost 200,000 years of wages that he was going to release him from the debt. After he was debt-free, the man ran into a fellow laborer who owed the newly forgiven man approximately three months wages. Unfortunately, the man did not extend a sampling of the mercy that the king offered to him. He threw his friend into prison even though there was a great probability that he would be paid back. The king found out that the forgiven man did not extend mercy to his fellow labor and called for the insensitive man to once again stand before him and give an account for his actions. And because the king was so upset that the man pardoned from his debt did not exhibit a similar level of mercy to his friend, the king required him to receive the severe punishment that was due him.

THE CHARACTER OF THE KING

What many thought was naivety, was actually an amazing display of mercy from the king. When he released the man, the king knew the man could never pay the insurmountable debt. And knowing that there was no possible way the man could ever be free from his financial debt, the king extended an unbelievable level of mercy toward the man and gave him a possibility to live the rest of his life debt-free. The ultimate point Jesus made in this parable (Matthew 18:23-35) is that God Himself is willing to release anyone from his/her insurmountable sin debt—a debt that no human being can ever pay off. The Lord extends His mercy to us so that we can get out from under the sin debt that would condemn our souls eternally. And in return, the Lord requires us to extend a sampling of His mercy to those around us.

"WHAT MANY THOUGHT WAS NAIVETY, WAS ACTUALLY AN AMAZING DISPLAY OF MERCY FROM THE KING."

The character of the king who demonstrated immeasurable levels of mercy toward one of his servants is a picture of God Himself. God is so extremely merciful that others have mocked Him for His commitment to extend mercy to those whom simply ask Him. The story of enormous mercy that we've seen in Matthew 18 is also elucidated in many other verses in the Bible

The Lord is more than justified to require us to be merciful people: (1) He is God and we should obey whatever He requires of us; (2) God Himself exhibits His mercy and compassion to each and every believer every single day of our lives. Mercy is at the heart of His Kingdom, and as Kingdom citizens we should exhibit the same level of mercy to those around us. There is no wonder that the writers of the Bible appeal to God's example of showing mercy to us as the motivation for us to live merciful lives towards those around us. Take a moment to meditate upon this small sampling of Bible verses listed below. Each one shares a uniquely beautiful perspective on God's mercy:

Ephesians 2:4a
But God, who is <u>rich in mercy</u> . . .

Lamentations 3:22-23
Through <u>the LORD's mercies we are not consumed</u>, because His compassions fail not. They are new every morning; Great is Your faithfulness.

Psalm 103:4
Who redeems your life from destruction, <u>Who crowns you with lovingkindness and tender mercies</u> . . .

2 Corinthians 1:3
Blessed be the God and Father of our Lord Jesus Christ, <u>the Father of mercies</u> and God of all comfort . . .

Psalm 23:6
Surely <u>goodness and mercy shall follow me all the days of my life</u>; And I will dwell in the house of the LORD forever.

Psalm 86:3-5
Be merciful to me, O Lord,
For I cry to You all day long.
Rejoice the soul of Your servant,
For to You, O Lord, I lift up my soul.

For You, <u>Lord, are good, and ready to forgi</u>
And <u>abundant in mercy</u> to all those who call

Hebrews 4:16
Let us therefore come boldly to the throne of g, *t we may*
<u>obtain mercy and find grace to help</u> in time of need <u>we may</u>

But amid the many beautiful Bible verses that comm, on God's
mercy, one of the most vivid descriptions of God's mercy is fo, n Psalm
103:

Psalm 103:8-12
<u>The LORD is merciful</u> and gracious,
  Slow to anger, and abounding in mercy.
He will not always strive with us,
  Nor will He keep His anger forever.
He has not dealt with us according to our sins,
  Nor punished us according to our iniquities.
For as the heavens are high above the earth,
  <u>So great is His mercy toward those who fear Him;</u>
As far as the east is from the west,
  So far has He removed our transgressions from us.

Take a moment to ponder all of the descriptive words about God's character. And as you do, compare His example to your own life to see in which ways you are honoring Him by living out these characteristics. Consider in which areas you could strengthen your own spiritual life.

> **"CONSIDER IN WHICH AREAS YOU COULD STRENGTHEN YOUR OWN SPIRITUAL LIFE."**

The Lord is . . .
- **merciful** (willing to withhold what we deserve)
- **gracious** (willing to grant us what we do not deserve)
- **slow to anger** (patient in order to promote repentance)

- **mercy** (exhibits mercy to a level beyond any other
- hum **going to strive with us** (won't continue to accuse us
  not er we repent)
- of o **g with us according to our sins** (does not hold our
  no lly against us)
- sin **ishing us according to our iniquities** (withholds the
  n e deserve)
- **eat in His mercy toward those who fear Him** (a promise
  at mercy towards His precious children)

d finally,

- **The Lord has "removed our transgressions from us"** (forgiven once and for all—His forgiveness is final!)

HAVE YOU EVER SAID, "THANKS?"

Have you ever taken the time to say, "Thanks" to the Lord for what He has done for you according to Psalm 103? Reexamine each phrase and recall a time that God has dealt with you in this fashion. Can you recall a time when the Lord withheld something you deserved? Or, when He allowed you to experience a blessing that you did not deserve? Was there a time where God was patient with you in order for you to come around and confess your sin rather than dropping His judgment upon you immediately? Have you ever had someone respond to you with continual mercy when everyone else around you did not want to give you a second chance? Have you been in a relationship where the other person did not continue to accuse you of your sin after you confessed and repented . . . and that individual also committed never to hold it against you in the future? It takes remembering that we have been recipients of God's unlimited mercy in order for us to remember to extend a sampling of that same limitless mercy to those around us. Only when we become people who promote mercy will God begin to use our lives to make an eternal impact upon the lives of others.

GOD USES MERCIFUL PEOPLE

God will use merciful people to be "change agents" in the lives of people within the body of Christ, as well as in the lives of those who are not yet within the Body. God will stop the forward progress of the proud, but He will lavish grace upon those who have been humbled by God's mercy to continue ministering to others around them (James 4:6). God deploys the merciful to speak His message of mercy to others. So the goal is to cultivate mercy deep down in your heart so that it becomes a conviction within your heart to be a merciful person toward others.

How is mercy learned? Well, for some, it's not been a real struggle because they have remained sensitive to what God's Word says about mercy, and they've been open to the Holy Spirit's work in their lives. For others, it may take a kaleidoscope of mistakes before they personally experience and understand God's loving mercy. Only then can they begin to show mercy to others. But regardless of how you have learned mercy in your life, be encouraged that once you understand the direct correlation between showing mercy and glorifying God, He will use your testimony and your words to bring glory to Him.

Recently a friend and I co-wrote a book that focuses on the true meaning of ministry. It is entitled *Ministry Is . . . How to Serve Jesus with Passion and Confidence.* In my preparation for the book, I meditated upon what I consider to be one of the most beautiful (and often overlooked) examples of boundless mercy. The remaining portion of this chapter is taken from chapter three of that writing project. It is the story of how one Christian man extended mercy to another man who at one point in his life exhibited nothing but hatred towards Christians.

A MAN IN NEED OF MERCY

God can make a minister out of anyone! Regardless of the mistakes, missteps, regrets, or past reputation of any person, the mercy of God provides a second chance. You may have been a blasphemer, scoffer, atheist, agnostic, doubter, or blatant sinner in your past, God can still use you to be a minister of the gospel.

But why would God use a person with such a sordid past? Why

"GOD CAN MAKE A MINISTER OUT OF ANYONE!"

doesn't He deploy only those who have seemingly never made any big mistakes in their lives? Why does He not mind that His spiritual army is full of people who have once demonstrated such horrible spiritual actions against Him?

The answer is simple: Who better to deliver the message of mercy than those who have personally experienced God's mercy! This is vividly testified in the life of a man named Sosthenes.

Sosthenes was considered a spiritual and social leader in the city of Corinth. He was responsible to facilitate not only religious training for the Jewish people in the first century but also the social activities that took place regularly in the synagogue. Even though he had been a student of the Old Testament and Jewish culture, he unfortunately did not accept the message of Jesus Christ as the true Messiah. When he heard of a minister named Paul who felt called by the living God to preach this gospel in his city, Sosthenes became outraged.

*After this, he left from Athens and went to Corinth . . . Then the Lord said to Paul in a night vision, "Don't be afraid, but keep on speaking and don't be silent. For I am with you, and no one will lay a hand on you to hurt you, because I have many people in this city." And he stayed there a year and six months, teaching the word of God among them (**Acts 18:1, 9-11** HCSB).*

In Sosthenes' desire to protect his tradition and beliefs, he grew hostile to the message of Jesus Christ and to those who purported such a "heretical" message," especially Paul. Sosthenes believed that the gospel message would convert the people of Corinth to a belief system contrary to his own. He also feared it would alter their social activities. Sosthenes' hatred for Paul escalated to the point that he physically detained Christians and pursued legal prosecution against them.

While Gallio was proconsul of Achaia, the Jews made a united attack against Paul and brought him to the judge's bench. "This man," they said, "persuades people to worship God contrary to the law" (*Acts 18:12-13* HCSB).

Sosthenes was passionate about putting an end to the propagation of the Christian message even if it meant the interrogation and castigation of the messenger. But just as Genesis 50:20 reminds us, God can take what some mean as evil and use it for good.

*And as Paul was about to open his mouth, Gallio said to the Jews, "If it were a matter of a crime or of moral evil, it would be reasonable for me to put up with you Jews. But if these are questions about words, names, and your own law, see to it yourselves. I don't want to be a judge of such things." So he drove them from the judge's bench. Then they all seized Sosthenes, the leader of the synagogue, and beat him in front of the judge's bench. But none of these things concerned Gallio (*Acts 18:14-17* HCSB).*

God protected His minister, Paul, during the attack of Sosthenes. Beyond that, God's mercy reached the heart of the attacker, Sosthenes. "How do we know this?" By some means God changed the life of Sosthenes between the beating at the end of the court battle in Acts 18 and the writing of I Corinthians. Maybe somehow underneath the pile of angry people, Sosthenes got some spiritual sense knocked into him and he began to run towards the truth of Christ—sort of a spiritual "hit and run!"

A MAN WHO RECEIVED MERCY

We are not told the specific details surrounding the conversion of Sosthenes to Christianity, but we have a pretty good idea which minister God used to reach this desperately sinful man. Notice the very first words of the first letter that the apostle Paul wrote after leaving the city of Corinth:

*Paul, called as an apostle of Christ Jesus by God's will, **and our brother Sosthenes** . . . (*1 Corinthians 1:1* HCSB, emphasis added).*

Amazing! Sosthenes became a recipient of God's mercy. He received God's mercy, confessed his sins, and experienced true salvation through Jesus Christ.

For what purpose could God possibly have for such a wretched man? What imaginable use could God have for such a blasphemous scoffer and flagrant persecutor of the gospel of Jesus Christ? Would a heart so callous ever be opened to the truth of the gospel? And if so, who would make an attempt to reach such a man?

The answer: Someone who was once a blasphemous scoffer and flagrant persecutor himself. Someone who has experienced the life-changing mercy of God for himself! I find it ironic in a way that the Lord brought the apostle Paul and Sosthenes together. For wasn't Paul himself a blasphemer to the tenth degree? So, why is a former persecutor of Christians (Paul) openly receiving a man who persecuted him? Answer: Paul extended mercy to Sosthenes because he personally experienced God's mercy. In Paul, Sosthenes experienced a bond that transcended human emotions and a sense of fairness. Paul exhibited mercy and was able to continue to minister with a man who at one time laid stripes upon his back and desired ill upon him.

A CITY IN NEED OF MERCY

Let's not stop with Sosthenes. Consider the entire city of Corinth to which Paul devoted over three and a half years of his life and to whom he wrote some of his longest and most detailed letters (1 & 2 Corinthians). The testimony of Sosthenes seems tranquil compared to the lifestyle of the citizens of Corinth. Still, God wanted to see these people come to Him and for them to experience His great mercy.

Corinth was not a godly city but rather a cesspool of sin and debauchery. It was commonly known in the first century that Corinth was a city known for immorality. Even their name became synonymous with living an immoral life. They worshiped false gods and involved themselves in inappropriate sexual activity all in the name of "worship" to their gods. Corinth was positioned on major travel routes, thus it attracted many transient people who were "here today and gone tomorrow." This only added to the temptation to indulge in immorality with the feeling of little to no consequence. Corinth harbored those whose lives were far from the Lord.

A CITY THAT RECEIVED MERCY

God loves sinners. He honed in on Corinth and instructed His ministers to infiltrate its' society because He desired for these people to come to Him. In fact, God specifically mandated Paul to personally go to Corinth and reach those people with the gospel. As we read earlier, the Lord spoke to Paul by a vision and sent Him specifically to Corinth (Acts 18:9) The Lord promised, "for I am with you, and no one is going to attack and harm you because I have many people in this city" (Acts 18:10). God desired that sinful men and women would experience His mercy!

Knowing this about the city of Corinth makes Paul's second verse in 1 Corinthians an even more magnificent testimony of God's mercy:

> To **the church** of God which is at Corinth, to those who are **sanctified** in Christ Jesus, called to be **saints**, with all who in every place call on the name of Jesus Christ our Lord, both theirs and ours. (*1 Corinthians 1:2*, emphasis added).

Did you catch the words used to describe these people? "Sanctified!" "Saints!" Better yet, "the church!" *And* they are considered one of us now—"with all who in every place call on the name of Jesus Christ our Lord, both theirs and ours!"

Why does God focus on those who need His mercy the most? Because these types of people comprise the membership of the church! The church is entirely made up of people who stood in the need of God's mercy and who have graciously received His forgiveness and cleansing.

"WHY DOES GOD FOCUS ON THOSE WHO NEED HIS MERCY THE MOST?"

Therefore, it seems that if the entire church is comprised by those who have been recipients of God's mercy, and it can only be populated by those who have admitted their need for the mercy of God, that the mission of every minister in the body of Christ should be a mission of extending God's great mercy to the world!

"AND SUCH WERE SOME OF YOU"

All of us are sinners (Romans 3:23) and all us deserve death and hell (Romans 6:23). Mercy is God's amazing kindness in not giving us the punishment and judgment we deserve.

In order to keep this in the forefront of every minister's mind, the Scriptures remind us that we were once no better spiritually than those to whom we are ministering. In the same letter to the church at Corinth, Paul provides us with this profound reminder of our past spiritual state:

> *Do you not know that the unjust will not inherit God's kingdom? Do not be deceived: no sexually immoral people, idolaters, adulterers, male prostitutes, homosexuals, thieves, greedy people, drunkards, revilers, or swindlers will inherit God's kingdom.* **Some of you were like this***; but you were washed, you were sanctified, you were justified in the name of the Lord Jesus Christ and by the Spirit of our God (**1 Corinthians 6:9-11** HCSB, emphasis added).*

Look at this listing—"sexually immoral people, idolaters, adulterers, male prostitutes, homosexuals, thieves, greedy people, drunkards, revilers, or swindlers." Note the transformation—"you were washed, you were sanctified, you were justified." Don't miss Paul's reminder—"and such were some of you." Effective ministry is remembering where you came from. It is remembering who you would be without Jesus Christ and His mercy.

"EFFECTIVE MINISTRY IS REMEMBERING WHERE YOU CAME FROM."

This reminder was not unique to the city of Corinth. Paul emphasizes this point to every group of believers with whom he came into contact.

Notice his words to the people who lived in Crete. In the First Century, Cretans were synonymous with barbaric behavior, brash and abrasive character, laziness, and habitual lying. Their culture was steeped in sin and depravity. Yet, God offered great mercy to these people as well:

For we too were once foolish, disobedient, deceived, captives of various passions and pleasures, living in malice and envy, hateful, detesting one another. **But when the goodness and love for man appeared from God our Savior, He saved us —not by works of righteousness that we had done, but according to His mercy,** *through the washing of regeneration and renewal by the Holy Spirit. This [Spirit] He poured out on us abundantly through Jesus Christ our Savior, so that having been justified by His grace, we may become heirs with the hope of eternal life* (**Titus 3:3-7** *HCSB, emphasis added*).

Consider Paul's letter to yet another church, Ephesus. Here he stresses the fact that all believers have received insurmountable levels of mercy from God:

And you He made alive, who were dead in trespasses and sins, in which you once walked according to the course of this world, according to the prince of the power of the air, the spirit who now works in the sons of disobedience, among whom also we all once conducted ourselves in the lusts of our flesh, fulfilling the desires of the flesh and of the mind, and were by nature children of wrath, just as the others. **But God, who is rich in mercy, because of His great love with which He loved us, even when we were dead in trespasses, made us alive together with Christ** *(by grace you have been saved), and raised us up together, and made us sit together in the heavenly places in Christ Jesus, that in the ages to come He might show the exceeding riches of His grace in His kindness toward us in Christ Jesus* (**Ephesians 2:1-7** *HCSB, emphasis added*).

What is real ministry? It is remembering that you have been the recipient of God's mercy and being a conveyor of that mercy to others.

DO YOU "LOVE MERCY"?

If those who live and work closely to you were asked to describe the way in which you disciple and discipline them, would they describe your actions as actions performed out of compassion and for their betterment? Or, would the question be met with feelings of frustration, unfairness, and an absence of sincere mercy?

Do people come to you willing to accept your tender words of correction and instruction because they believe you will deliver those words in a merciful spirit? Or have you grown to appreciate uninterrupted office hours and a weekly schedule devoid of visits and phone calls from fellow believers because they do not wish to experience your abrasive tone and merciless counsel? I beseech you to pause right now and really do some self-evaluation.

Ask yourself the tough questions in order to minister in the spirit that God requires of every minister. Then, take a moment to ask significant people in your life (i.e. roommates, close friends, wife, husband, children, co-workers, etc.) to evaluate you as a person of mercy. Provide them the opportunity to speak freely without interruption about how they perceive you, your actions, your counsel, and your responses to them. Tell them that you relish their honesty in order to become a better minister. If you do this, I'll make this prediction—you will witness in their replies to you a true demonstration of tender mercy.

I also want to encourage you to memorize the following Scripture verse and recite it regularly on your way into class or to work, before you return home, and as you prepare to minister to those under your care. Rehearse its teaching during a busy season of your life. Recount its truths right in the middle of a conversation with a loved one that has all the makings of becoming "heated." Place it in the frame of a mirror that you frequent during the mornings and evenings at your home. Teach it to those around you so that they can help you live according to its truths. But most of all make the truths of this verse the deep desire of your heart as a minister:

> *He has shown you, O man, what is good; And what does the LORD require of you but to do justly, to love mercy, and to walk humbly with your God? (**Micah 6:8**).*

WRITE IT DOWN:

Mercy is at the heart of God's kingdom. As a believer, the Lord has extended His mercy and compassion to you every single day of your life. Does God expect any less of us? Think about those merciful people who God has used as "change agents in your life. Why not encourage their hearts today with a note of thanks for the mercy they showed you at the particular time when you needed it? You will make their day!

How can you "pay it forward?" Think of specific people that need an extra measure of mercy from you today. List their names below, and write down how you plan to pour out God's mercy on them. The more specific you are, the more likely you will follow through in extending them mercy!

NOTES

FIVE
Walk Humbly

CHAPTER FIVE: *Walk Humbly*

This is one of the hardest guiding spiritual principles to learn in any Christian's life. To "Do Justly" and "Love Mercy" may take some discipline to cultivate, but to **"Walk Humbly"** will be a spiritual principle that will take each one of us a lifetime to master. It also requires a daily regimen of reminders to stay on track. But the believer that strives to walk in humility (i.e. total dependence upon God) every day will find that it provides a level of unparalleled peace in his or her heart. And the result will be God-honoring respect for those with whom they interact.

> **"...TO 'WALK HUMBLY' WILL BE A SPIRITUAL PRINCIPLE THAT WILL TAKE EACH ONE OF US A LIFETIME TO MASTER."**

The Lord requires us to live humble lives just as He requires us to "Do Justly" and "Love Mercy." And again, we do not get a choice of whether or not we want to be a humble person. We are reminded in Micah 6:8 that humility "is good," and therefore, it is valuable, necessary, and appropriate conduct for all believers.

Micah 6:8

He has shown you, O man, what is good; and what does the LORD require of you but to do justly, to love mercy, and to walk humbly with your God?

IT GOES DEEPER THAN WORDS

"Walk Humbly" is the third guiding spiritual principle listed in Micah 6:8 that every believer should adopt in order to bring glory to God. Humility serves as a filter for all of us as we function together within the body of Christ. Walking humbly has everything to do with conditioning your heart to be sensitive to holiness as you perform selfless acts of kindness to others. If the heart is conditioned to be humble and dependent upon God, then the mouth (i.e. actions) will naturally follow:

Luke 6:45
A good man out of the good treasure of his heart brings forth good; and an evil man out of the evil treasure of his heart brings forth evil. For out of the abundance of the heart his mouth speaks.

A BIG GIFT IN A SMALL PACKAGE

There is a short verse in the book of Philippians that speaks about how to develop a heart of humility and how to exhibit that humility to those around you.

Philippians 2:3
Let nothing be done through selfish ambition or conceit, but in lowliness of mind let each esteem others better than himself.

In this small verse, we will learn some profound yet intensely practical lessons regarding humility. Just as Micah 6:8 instructs us clearly on how to live a life that brings glory to God, Philippians 2:3 provides crystal clear guidance on how to live a humble life and how to safeguard from pride entering our lives. Some time ago, I drafted several specific thoughts on this issue of humility, and in 2011 those thoughts were published in my book, *Living Out the Mind of Christ - Practical Keys to Discovering and Applying the Mind of Christ in Everyday Life*. The following is taken from an abridged portion of that book. I encourage you to take time to mediate upon the following exposition of Philippians 2:3. Cultivate its teaching in your own heart first, and then teach its principles to those with whom you worship God.

TAKING A CLOSE LOOK

In Philippians 2:3, the words "lowliness of mind" are taken from the apostle Paul's use of one word that literally means "low thinking," "humble thinking," or "in a humble mindset." It is clear from this verse that humility is the second of three attitudes that comprise the mind of Christ. Therefore, if you want to live out the mind of Christ in your church, home, and relationships, you must also demonstrate the attitude of biblical humility.

A good way to look at this verse is to first examine everything before the words "lowliness of mind [humility]" before you focus on the second half of the verse. We do this because the verse follows an orderly and logical format. The first half of the verse offers two "sinful attitudes" that will prevent you from living your life in humility. After identifying these sinful attitudes, the verse then prescribes a spiritual activity that will safeguard us from having pride creep into our lives.

TWO SINFUL ATTITUDES

Philippians 2:3a
Let nothing be done through selfish ambition or conceit . . .

This first portion of the verse allows no room for these two attitudes to be resident in the heart of a humble person. There are absolutely no exceptions to this command—no negotiations on the matter—no compromise—no safe limit is put on these attitudes in the heart of a believer. In addition, there are no imaginable circumstances that would warrant the adoption of these two attitudes in any discussion, consideration or action in a believer's life. That is why the verse says let "*nothing*" be done through these attitudes. In fact, when the apostle Paul penned these words, he wrote the word "*nothing*" twice in this sentence! It is emphasized in this verse that we cannot have the sinful attitudes of selfish ambition or conceit if we want to live out the mind of Christ.

Sinful Attitude #1 –
"SELFISH AMBITION" – A SELF-PROMOTING HEART

"*Selfish ambition*" implies that one is doing something for the sole purpose of promoting himself and not the glory of God. These two words, "*selfish ambition,*" offer a translation for the one word that the apostle Paul used when he penned this verse. The word Paul chose was actually a word used of politicians who would travel from town to town for the purpose of soliciting people's votes of support! Admittedly, there may be a purpose for this type of action in politics when election season is upon us, but there is no room for this type of selfish promotion within the body of Christ.

Therefore, Philippians 2:3 teaches that if you desire to minister in the attitude of humility, you cannot for any reason follow the path of self-promotion. In my personal observation, those who attempt to promote themselves in ministry stick out like a sore thumb! It does not take much discernment to pick a self-promoter out of a crowd. Regardless of the tact, people skills, courtesies, spiritual activity or jargon used by these individuals, their motives are obvious.

Why do self-promoters eventually reveal themselves to everyone? Because the ones who desire to promote themselves begin to deceive themselves. They believe that they are better at disguising their motives than they really are! And regardless of all the careful planning, preparing, and creative speech writing of a self-promoter, a shadow of doubt is cast in the minds of spiritual people. Remember, God's Word is likened to "light." And if you saturate yourself with the Word of God, you are going to be able to discern anything that is not light. Even though some sins seem transparent so as not to cast a shadow in the presence of light, the spiritually sensitive person will ultimately be able to identify anything that casts even a faint shadow.

Sinful Attitude #2 –
"CONCEIT" – AN INFLATED EGO

"*Conceit*" is a word that means "empty accolades and opinions" of man. When the apostle Paul penned this verse, he used a compound word that literally means "empty glory" or "empty opinions." In other words—an inflated ego or conceit is the result of listening to and depending upon the empty praise of man.

Every believer in Jesus Christ needs to be careful not to get ensnared in the trap of listening to the praises of man and believing those empty opinions—whether they come from your family, your friends or your church community. Pastors, in particular, may even get to the point of formulating their sermons based on what will produce the very accolades that this verse warns about. You may find yourself driving home after a Sunday morning service contemplating a "better way" to preach that will result in more accolades. Don't be deceived. Check the motive of your heart. When your only desire is that the Lord receives all the glory and praise, it is irrelevant whether you receive any accolades.

God will sustain you with His encouragement, which is neither empty nor fleeting. How does He do this? By informing you of *eternal* results! In His perfect time, you will learn of a member of your congregation who has accepted

"DON'T BE DECEIVED. CHECK THE MOTIVE OF YOUR HEART."

Christ after contemplating what you shared from God's Word. You will hear of a father beginning the baby-steps of change in order to be the spiritual leader in his home. You will receive word of a young child who has made a God-honoring choice in school because of what God has done through your influence. These are the eternal rewards for which we labor!

If these two sinful attitudes are resident within your heart, biblical humility is impossible, and subsequently you are unable to live out the mind of Christ. Now that we understand that selfish ambition and conceit will prevent a believer from living in humility, let's look at a biblical safeguard that can help us maintain a humble spirit in order to live out the mind of Christ.

A BIBLICAL SAFEGUARD

Philippians 2:3b
. . . *but in lowliness of mind let each esteem others better than himself.*

This latter portion of Philippians 2:3 offers a biblical safeguard to anyone who desires to live out the attitude of humility. The safeguard is distinctly stated in the verse and does not require much clarification. The verse simply builds on the previous teaching that our flesh will naturally want to promote ourselves. Selfish ambition and conceit give our minds the confidence to believe that we are better than others. So the verse recommends the following safeguard to maintain an attitude of humility. Whenever you interact with a person, your initial thought should be that he or she is better than you!

There is one word in this statement that is key to grasping the vividness of this safeguard. Notice the word "esteem." In the language of the apostle Paul, this word meant "*better*" or "*more significant.*" So, in order to keep our minds humble and protected from becoming "holier than thou," we should consider our time interacting with others as a privilege and an honor—and we should let them know that we feel this way! One way of demonstrating this is to acknowledge the strengths and accomplishments of others. Even though you may have more credentials, more experience, more authority, or a greater aptitude in certain subjects, make the effort to focus on their interests, passions and strengths—NOT out of a prideful pity for them but out of sincere appreciation for them!

The apostle Paul actually practiced this principle before he recommended it in Philippians 2:3b. Notice the very first verse in the book of Philippians and how Paul began this letter:

Philippians 1:1
Paul and Timothy, bondservants of Jesus Christ, To all the saints in Christ Jesus who are in Philippi, with the bishops and deacons.

Paul refers to the recipients of this letter by their official and authoritative titles, "*bishops*" and "*deacons.*" Observe, though, the way Paul refers to himself, "Paul and Timothy, *bondservants* of Jesus Christ." What is interesting is that Paul did not apply to himself his most authoritative (and most frequently used) title, "Apostle." He referred to himself as a "servant." He exalted their rightful position as Christian leaders of the church of Philippi and esteemed them as spiritual leaders while he deemphasized his role in the church. In humility, Paul did so to take the attention off of his leadership role. Did the people realize the significance of what Paul did in Philippians 1:1? Not immediately. But when they got to Philippians 2:3, I am sure they paused and reflected on the opening sentence of the entire book.

Why did Paul do this? Because he was not about to recommend others to do something that he was not willing to do himself! Paul first practiced in Philippians 1:1 what he eventually preached in Philippians 2:3. Likewise, regardless of how smart, articulate, educated, affluent or involved in ministry you are, you must view those around you just as our

Lord and Creator views them—as valuable and precious creations of God. And considering them as such will assist you maintaining an attitude of humility.

THE ENEMY OF HUMILITY IS PRIDE

It is curious that this is the only attitude that the Bible offers a recommended safeguard. I believe the reason is because pride is a relentless sin. It never takes a rest in its attempt to dissuade our attention from the glory of God and turn our eyes upon "ME." Genesis 4:7 reminds us that the temptation to sin is deceitful and ruthless when it says "... if you do not do well, sin lies at the door. And its desire *is* for you, but you should rule over it." Sin crouches low at the doorway, observing when the opportune time is to persuade you to turn away from following God's way. And if you feel that you are not affected by its craftiness or feel as if you are immune to its influences, please take great caution! This is not a positive commentary on your impressive spiritual maturity, but rather a negative commentary regarding your desensitized discernment. The idea that you are immune to sin's influence makes you open prey to the devastating power of your prideful flesh. The way in which the Devil seeks to "steal, and to kill, and to destroy" (John 10:10) is often not through some physical, cataclysmic, accident, but through the subtle yet influential lies of the flesh that daily "war against the soul" (1 Peter 2:11). It is not *weakness* to acknowledge the daily safeguards that you must implement in order to protect you from your flesh—it is *wisdom*!

Man's applause is addictive. Self-promotion is like a drug in that, if you taste the results of your self-promoting efforts, your flesh will drool at the opportunity for more. And once hooked on the taste of pride, you might as well pull out your calendar and plan on the end of your ministry because God promises that He will stop the forward progress of prideful people. The Bible is clear about this promise.

> "MAN'S APPLAUSE IS ADDICTIVE. SELF-PROMOTION IS LIKE A DRUG ..."

In James 4:6b, the Bible says "*God resists the proud, but gives grace to the humble.*" Notice in this verse that it says that God "*resists*" the proud. In today's world, this could take on several different meanings. For example, when many people go on a diet, they attempt to "resist" the temptation to eat certain foods. In this example, the word "resist" could mean "ignore the advances of" or "get angry about." So, does James 4:6b teach that God will only ignore or get angry at those who live in pride? No. Pride is a much more serious offense to God for Him not to act upon it.

What is interesting is that when the apostle Peter penned this verse, he used a unique word for the word "*resist*" that actually means "to stand against." In fact, the apostle Paul borrows this word and uses it four times in his description for the armor of God in Ephesians 6:10-14a. Notice the four occurrences in this passage where the word "stand" appears. Each word that is translated "stand" is taken from the very same word that the apostle Peter used for the word "*resist*" in James 4:6:

Ephesians 6:10-14a
Finally, my brethren, be strong in the Lord and in the power of His might. Put on the whole armor of God, that you may be able to stand against the wiles of the devil. For we do not wrestle against flesh and blood, but against principalities, against powers, against the rulers of the darkness of this age, against spiritual hosts of wickedness in the heavenly places. Therefore take up the whole armor of God, that you may be able to withstand in the evil day, and having done all, to stand. Stand therefore . . .

Therefore, God will not simply ignore the ones who exhibit the attitude of pride. God will not just be angry or frustrated at the ones who display a prideful attitude. He will not simply withhold blessings from the proud. Rather, God will "*stand against*" the proud. *He will stop the forward progress of the proud!* He will place a bulwark in front of the proud by which to halt any further progress of those who decide to minister with a prideful heart. The Scriptures are replete with statements that warn us of this inevitable outcome. The following verses should be etched in our memories as we attempt to live out the mind of Christ in our families, relationships and ministries:

Proverbs 16:18
Pride goes before destruction, and a haughty spirit before a fall.

Galatians 6:7
Do not be deceived, God is not mocked; for whatever a man sows, that he will also reap.

1 Corinthians 5:6-7a
Your glorying is not good. Do you not know that a little leaven leavens the whole lump? Therefore purge out the old leaven . . ."

Remember this principle: Pride is a weapon that enjoys destroying people's lives. Pride plays no favorites. Pride will turn on you just as quickly as it clung to you upon your summoning it to be your partner in ministry. Pride will destroy your ministry!

"PRIDE WILL DESTROY YOUR MINISTRY"

It is hard to know why the Lord allows some to continue in their pride as they live their lives and even minister as Christian Leaders. But be assured of this truth: there will be a time when God will deal with the sin of pride in every person's life. Therefore, our thoughts and prayers should not be about the destruction of a prideful person— "God, when you punish them, punish them hard!" No, our prayers should be about restoring him/her—"God, give this person the wisdom to repent from their sinful way before it leads to destruction."

MY TESTIMONY

I personally believe that every minister—whether musician, technician, preacher, or teacher— has to grapple with the pride issue at some time in their lives. I believe there must be a point and time in which every minister must decide once and for all for whose glory they will minister. My prayer is that you will decide early (and remind yourself often) that you will usher all praise, all glory, and all honor to the One who has given you the very ability to influence others and minister in your present capacity. For me, I confronted the issue of pride in the last semester of my undergraduate year.

I remember as a college student, in the last semester of my undergraduate program, I was excited to enter seminary. I had planned on working hard to finish strong in the remaining semester as an undergraduate. Yet, my sights were eagerly anticipating the day when I would be able to graduate from seminary and get into full-time ministry. I took consolation in that all of my friends felt the same way, as we often dreamed together about the day we would all be in full-time ministry. I remember one conversation in the cafeteria that forever changed my perspective on dreaming about working in ministry.

As my friends and I sat around the cafeteria table we began talking about ministry. I anticipated a lot of "futurist" talk about full-time ministry, but I was surprised to hear that four of my friends had made plans to enter ministry in a matter of a couple months. I listened intently as I heard one of them say that the four had discussed their desire to minister together, and they were making plans to approach a major denominational association to consider funding their church planting efforts. I was somewhat shocked at this news but also excited to hear of the new developments. So, they proceeded to elaborate on their ministry plan to me. It started out pretty exciting and God-honoring; then it turned into something that rattled me to my core. The dialogue went as follows (paraphrased with changed names):

> We were all just hanging around and then it finally hit us: 'If we like to hang out together, why don't we minister with each other?' So, we decided to minister together. And check this out – we realized that each of our giftedness fits every major area of ministry. John is the best singer at our school right now, so he can do worship. Ken is the best youth guy here, so he can head up the student ministries. Steve is the best administrator of anyone I know, so he could be the administrative pastor. And the guys tell me that I am the best preacher so I could be the Senior Pastor. What a team, huh? Also, we have learned that there are no mega churches in the Dakota's, so we are all going to leave after we graduate with our undergrad degrees and go out there and plant the state's first mega church! What do you think?!

I was stunned. I think my friend kept on talking because I remember hearing vibrations of conversation as if they were faint background noises, but I don't think I responded to his question. It was as if my mind focused on the phrase, "*We are going to plant the state's first mega church!*" I walked back to my dorm room thinking, "Is that right?!" "How can anyone *predetermine* that you are going to build a mega church?" I thought God was the One who determined this type of result. Then my mind reflected on all the people who gave credence to their plan and commended it as if they knew beyond a shadow of a doubt that God was going to bless it even more than they had planned! At the same time, I wondered if my numb reaction was because everyone else now had clarity as to their future career and I didn't' yet know what I was going to do or where I was going to minister. I wanted their ambition, yet at the same time I felt like there was something wrong with the way they were going about it. I was confused.

Later that evening, I remember remaining in my dorm room to study. My roommate was gone so I had some uninterrupted time. Yet, my mind was not on my studies as it drifted to the conversation that I had heard earlier in the day. I wasn't in the mood to go out with my friends or participate in the many weekend school-sponsored activities. I just wanted to be alone with my thoughts and God. I believe it was God's way of causing me to confront the very important question that every minister has to confront at some point in their ministerial career—"*What place will pride have in my ministry?*"

I remember rehearsing the words of my friend from our lunchtime conversation. They resonated in my mind over and over as if they were building to a crescendo:

"We are going to plant the state's first mega church!"
"I'm the best preacher...!"
"He's the best singer...!"
"He's the best...!"
"He's the best...!"
"What do you think, Ben?"
"We are going to plant the state's first mega church!"
"We are going to plant...!"
"He's the best preacher...!"

"What do you think, Ben?"
"We are going to plant a mega church...!"
"WE are...!"
"WE are...!"
"WE ARE...!"

"God forbid!" I shouted as I immediately fell to the floor and knelt near the lower bunk and cried out to God:

"God, Help me! I know it is wrong yet I am jealous of my friends because it sounds like they are going to be so far ahead of me! My flesh, oh God, is telling me, "Why don't you see if you can get on their team?" So many people are going to talk about them, support them, and tout that they are the examples for all other ministry students to follow! Help me, God, because my flesh says one thing...but my spirit is scared to ever say I can do anything in my own power without You. God, shut down my flesh! Help me never to make plans outside of Your will for my life! I mean it, God. Help me trust You because my flesh makes it look really good and tells me that I can trust my own wisdom. Help me! It is hard to trust You sometimes. I am sorry that it is. Help me!"

Then I will never forget the promise I offered to God:

"God, I will make You a promise. From this day forward, I will promise You that I will work as hard as I can. I will strive to do the best at what I can do to demonstrate to You how serious I am about using the gifts You have given me for Your glory. And I will lean totally on You IF You want to lift me up. If You want to lift me up – then so be it. If You don't allow me to minister right now, then so be it. But I will strive to do my best for Your glory, and I promise to rest entirely on You. You decide to what levels of influence I should be lifted up."

I remember getting up off the floor feeling as if a huge weight had been lifted from my heart. No longer did I feel like I had to worry about monitoring my friends' progress or attempting to control the progress of other people. No longer did I feel that I had to compare my career path to the progress of someone else. For the first time in my life, I felt secure with where I was in the will of God. I realized that His will was not contingent on knowing where I was going to work or what the specific circumstances were surrounding my future ministry. Clarity and peace came when I trusted God and stopped listening to the lies that my prideful flesh was preaching to me.

Approximately a week later, God brought to my attention a life verse that often reminds me of that night of prayer in my dorm room. In fact, it is rare that I do not quote this verse in my prayer prior to a sermon, lesson, or lecture. That's because I want to hear its truths every time before I preach, teach, lecture, or write about the Word of God. I will open up my sermons, lessons, devotions, by quoting 1 Corinthians 2:4-5:

> [Lord, I pray that] my speech and my preaching [be] not with persuasive words of human wisdom, but in demonstration of the Spirit and of power, [so] that [our] faith should not [stand] in the wisdom of men but in the power of God.

I attempt to keep this prayer ever before my eyes. In every classroom, every preaching sermon, and in every writing project, I remember that if my goal is to write or preach so as to draw attention to my own skill and accomplishments, my wisdom will be faulty and my words will be weak. Further, my attempt to impact people's lives and to bring about eternal change will be futile. But I am persuaded that if I allow the Word of God to be prominent in my speech, if I get out of the way and allow the simple truths of the gospel to present its own case, if I determine that any emotions, gestures, or mannerisms that I display when I preach will be generated due to a deep passion for the subject matter and not for mere performance or to solicit an emotional reaction, that is the time where I will see God demonstrate His life-changing power through me!

Following that fateful evening of prayer, I have rested well in my ministry pursuits knowing that: God knows everything; God will lift up whom He desires to lift up; and God will protect me, my testimony, and my opportunities to work in His ministry just as long as I usher all praise to Him and rely on His way to accomplish His will!

HOW TO RECEIVE/GIVE A COMPLIMENT

As you make your decision to do all that you can in your ministry to ensure that all glory, praise, and honor is ushered to the Lord Jesus Christ, you will undoubtedly rehearse many different ways to make sure that you function in

"GOD WILL LIFT UP WHOM HE DESIRES TO LIFT UP. . ."

the spirit of humility. One of the commonly asked questions of those who are involved in any level of public ministry is, "How should I receive a compliment about something that I have said or done in my ministry?" There are effective ways to respond to a compliment that will help draw their attention to God and His Scriptures.

I encourage you to respond to a compliment by asking the person giving it to tell you the ways in which the Holy Spirit spoke to them during your speech, Bible lesson, devotional, prayer, or sermon. After receiving a compliment, consider asking, "What did God teach you during our time together?" "What did the Holy Spirit impress on your heart as you studied His Word?" "What Scriptures in particular moved you during the Bible lesson and why?" After they respond, take a moment to reflect on the Scriptures with them by possibly agreeing with them: "Yes, I too was moved when I read that in God's Word. It is a powerful verse, isn't it?" "You know, when I was studying for this sermon, God spoke so clearly to me about that very point of application as well. God is good, isn't He?" These types of responses will draw their attention to God and His Word—where the attention should be.

Conversely, if you personally have appreciated someone's ministry and you feel compelled to thank them for all the hard work and their sensitivity to the Holy Spirit as they ministered to the church/you, I recommend that you thank them in the way the apostle Paul thanked people in his writings. For example, notice all of the occasions listed below wherein the apostle Paul "thanked" people:

Philippians 1:3
I thank my God upon every remembrance of you.

Colossians 1:3
We give thanks to the God and Father of our Lord Jesus Christ, praying always for you.

1 Thessalonians 1:2a
We give thanks to God always for you all . . .

2 Thessalonians 1:3a
We are bound to thank God always for you, brethren . . .

Question: How many times did the apostle Paul thank "people" in the above verses?
ANSWER: ZERO!

The point is, Paul ushered all thanksgiving to the One who is the Giver of spiritual gifts, ministers, pastors, and friends! Paul was quick to say, "I thank GOD for you!" I have no doubt that every spirit-controlled minister will love to hear the compliment, "I thank God for you" coming from the lips of his parishioners or friends.

Admittedly, there is nothing wrong with simply saying "thank you" to a friend. But because we are currently discussing the issue of spiritual safeguards, I caution you to remember that your flesh is relentless in its attempt to look for any occasion to instill a sense of confidence within you. For me, therefore, I am not comfortable stringing together too many "thank you's" after a sermon without inserting that ever-important reminder of the One who is the Giver of the talent, skill, and giftedness.

FALSE HUMILITY VS. TRUE HUMILITY

But, watch out! Even if you do respond to a compliment in a God-focused manner, even in the same manner the apostle Paul thanked people; this will not solve every pride issue in your life. Remember, it is not the words that make a response reflect the attitude of humility; it is always the *heart* behind the words. You can say the very same words and bring attention to yourself rather than bring attention to God.

How do you know the difference between false humility and true humility? Words spoken in false humility sound humble on the surface, but in some subtle or obvious way they draw all attention to the person and not to God. True humility, on the other hand, can utilize the very same words in such a way to deflect any accolades that would only fuel pride and usher all the attention to God. Admittedly, it is challenging to describe this very fine line on paper, but I believe that if you have ever grappled with your prideful flesh in the past, you understand this fine line and the need to daily (albeit moment by moment) put to death the deeds of the flesh (Romans 8:12-14).

WHAT ABOUT YOU?

In order to know that you are living out the attitude of biblical humility, you must first examine your life and make sure that two sinful attitudes are eradicated in your life – a self-promoting heart and an inflated ego. These sinful attitudes are removed through confession and a concerted focus toward doing whatever it takes to safeguard you from stealing glory from God.

In order to maintain the attitude of humility, you must also be mindful of the damage that pride can cause in your life and ministry. Pride plays no favorites and it will cling to you if you open your heart to its lies; it can only destroy your testimony. Therefore, your focus should be on what brings about eternal rewards and glory to God. Following the teachings on Philippians 2:3 on humility, you can praise the Lord that He has provided you with perfect guidance through His Word to know that you are living a biblically humble life!

WRITE IT DOWN:

What are the two attitudes that must be removed in your life in order for you to demonstrate biblical humility? Spend some time to examine your own heart and identify the areas where these two prideful attitudes exist. (It's really not a matter of "if" they exist but "where" those thoughts have crept into your life.) Ask the Lord to demolish these prideful attitudes and give you a heart of humility.

Don't be deceived—pride plays no favorites and it will destroy your ministry. What safeguard to pride does Philippians 2:3 offer to anyone who desires to live out the attitude of humility? Write down how you will put this safeguard into practice in your daily interactions with others. There's no doubt—it will take PRACTICE!

NOTES

SIX

Serve Others

CHAPTER SIX: *Serve Others*

Before we can talk about evangelistic efforts and how to articulate our faith to others, we must first focus on the condition of our hearts. You see, if we are not in line with the Holy Spirit, our efforts will be empty and ultimately fruitless.

I recently had an individual approach me, and I remember vividly what he said, "If someone needs to get on fire for God, wouldn't it be beneficial to get him involved in ministry or in a leadership role? Then he could taste and see that the Lord is good!" The first thing that came to my mind was, "No – not a good idea! But I restrained myself. When this question was raised, the person was essentially saying that it might be profitable to put someone in a church "doing" position in order to get his or her heart fired up for God. I believe that's a prescription for failure because it's in reverse order. Scripture makes it very clear that prior to *doing* the work of ministry, first our hearts must be spiritually prepared.

In Acts 6:3 we see where the disciples were instructed by Paul to meet the needs of widows. He stated, "Therefore, brethren, seek out from among you seven men of good reputation, full of the Holy Spirit and wisdom, whom we may appoint over this business." Prior to dealing with the business at hand, the men needed to be spiritual, controlled, and in line with God. Before they could "do," their hearts needed to "be" ready.

> **"SCRIPTURE MAKES IT VERY CLEAR THAT PRIOR TO DOING THE WORK OF MINISTRY, FIRST OUR HEARTS MUST BE SPIRITUALLY PREPARED."**

I also think of 2 Timothy 2:2 where Paul says to Timothy, "And the things that you have heard from me among many witnesses, commit these to faithful men who will be able to teach others also." In other words, "Don't commit these things in order to make them faithful, but find men who are committed, who are spiritually mature and then commit these things to them." Paul wanted the mentors to find mentees who were already somewhat mature – men who saw their need for spiritual growth.

By examining these passages we see that today's Christians need to be similarly prepared to do ministry. Therefore, I don't want to jump right into evangelism without first addressing *who* we should be. This is a very important element of Christian service.

I was told at the first Bible college I attended that our personal devotion time should be comprised of material outside of our class studies, and we were encouraged to take time to talk to godly men who could influence our walk with Christ. One author of more than forty books who came to our school (the late John Wolford) made this statement, "I do not find myself getting the most out of God's Word unless I'm preparing to write a book, or preparing to preach a sermon or a lesson." He was saying, "If I'm not studying for a purpose, it's hard to get something out of it." I agreed with him that I should make my studies my devotion, studying for knowledge, application and life-change.

For you, I think the Lord has seen fit to expose you to the subjects of personal spiritual growth and evangelism at this particular time in your life. I pray that you will be able to use your times in God's Word as a tool to develop personal devotion and to examine your heart. In fact, if your mind is truly meditating on these spiritual truths, I believe you will learn great ways to apply these principles to your life as your heart is infused with His precious Word.

BEFORE I DO, I MUST BE

There are many misconceptions about what a godly person is. Many people refer to others as being "spiritual." For example, I have heard students recommend a girl to a friend as a potential date because "she's really a godly person." Or you may hear someone say, "You ought to consider dating him because he really loves the Lord." However, it is a likely possibility that the person being recommended is not a godly person in the true sense.

We are going to search God's Word to find a clear description of a godly person. As believers who desire to be holy before God, we need to make sure we understand how God defines a "godly person."

MISCONCEPTIONS ABOUT BEING A GODLY PERSON

They Have Biblical Training (Isaiah 29:13, NASB)

Some people describe a godly person as one who has received formal Bible training. Let's look at Isaiah 29:13, "Then the Lord said, 'Because this people draw near with their words and honor Me with their lip service, but they remove their hearts far from Me, and their reverence of Me consists of tradition learned by rote . . .'" Let me paraphrase: "They know a lot about Me and do lip service to Me, but their hearts are moved away from Me because their worship of Me is made up only of rules taught by men." Literally, they have learned God's precepts by empty rote memorization and have essentially flash-carded God's attributes to death without their heart being linked in devotion to Him.

Many people sit through years of Sunday school classes; they know the stories in their heads, but they do not apply them to their hearts. They may have perfect church attendance, they may have earned badges and memorized verses, but these disciplines usually will not produce a godly person in and of itself. It's all for show. According to Isaiah, the truths of God must be received into the heart and then lived out, regardless of any formal biblical training.

I was at a men's retreat in Jonesboro, Georgia with a fellow pastor, talking about integrity and purity among the men there. In a Q&A session, one of the men asked, "How is it that some pastors who preach the Word week in and week out can fall into adultery?" I responded, "I believe it's often because those pastors prepare sermons in second and third person. They say 'he' must do this, 'the church' must do that, and 'you' must do this. But prior to preaching, he needs to speak it in first person. He must say, 'I' must do this, or how can 'I' conform my life to this portion of God's Word?" Pastors and trained Bible students will fail when their training and preparation is not internalized. When they just go through the motions to prepare a sermon, it ends up being all for show. You see, if you tout how many books and volumes you have on your shelf but your heart is not holy, then the books are mere showpieces. So we see that it is not biblical training that necessarily prepares a person to be "godly." So it must be something else.

They Attend Church (Matthew 7)

In Matthew chapter 7 we read that on Judgment Day, "Many will say to Me in that day, 'Lord, Lord, have we not prophesied in Your name, cast out demons in Your name, and done many wonders in Your name?'" Notice that many of the things they named off were good things that they did for God. I know this passage is somewhat debatable because some say these people are believers, while some say they are not. If they are believers, they've done incredibly spiritual things: performing miracles, casting out demons, etc. Yet, the Bible says, "And then I will declare to them, 'I never knew you; depart from Me, you who practice lawlessness!'"

Some suggest these people are unbelievers who hung around in church and knew how to use the Christian vernacular in an attempt to persuade God to let them into heaven. They "talk the talk" but it's all empty. Regardless of who these individuals are, we see through their example that we must achieve more than a mere intellectual understanding of God; we must have more than just a cognitive knowledge of Him. There is a saying that twenty percent of the church does eighty percent of the work. We typically view the twenty percent as godly people, but a godly person must be about more than just work. In the Third Epistle of John, we see the story of a guy named Diotrephes. John says in 3 John verse 9, "I wrote to the church, but Diotrephes, who loves to have the preeminence (first place) among them does not receive us." We don't know if this man was a pastor or not, but we know he wanted to be; he wanted to be the leader.

In Colossians 1:18, we are told that Jesus Christ "is the head of the body, the church, who is the beginning, the firstborn from the dead, that in all things He may have the preeminence." If you want first place in the church solely for your own glory, you're going toe-to-toe with Jesus Christ. And so we see that Diotrephes was off track. Deeds performed in church or profound actions do not gain prominence with God.

In Matthew 13 we read the parable of the four soils. Seed is thrown on soil and some of it takes root and is then snatched away. Some hits bedrock and dies. Some is trampled on and there is no growth. And some hits the fine soil. These examples of soil represent non-believers. In like manner, some people show the likeness of a true believer but have no true grounding so that when things get tough they wither away.

They Have Spiritual Parents

Another misconception is that if we have spiritual parents we too will be automatically spiritual. I recall after my wife and I got married, she was sharing the gospel with a woman who was not a believer yet. She said, "Oh, I'm going to heaven." My wife replied, "Really? How do you know you're on your way to heaven?" The woman said, "Because my mother washes the parish priest's robes every week, and it takes a very special person to do this." My wife found her response sad as she was relying on her mother to gain spirituality.

In Philippians 3:4-5, Paul addressed this type of belief when he said, "If anyone else thinks he may have confidence in the flesh, I more so: circumcised the eighth day of the stock of Israel, of the tribe of Benjamin, a Hebrew of the Hebrews." This is a comment about his family and their wealth and standing in the Jewish community. The best teacher in Tarsus, Gamaliel, educated him. But then Paul goes on to say, "But what things were gain to me, these I have counted loss for Christ" (3:7).

Paul considered and weighed the worth of all that he had and all that he was and, like an accountant weighing assets and liabilities, he no longer considered them an asset. To Paul, they were of no worth in comparison to knowing Christ. So as we are weighing these different things – biblical training, church attendance, and spiritual parents – we need to continue our biblical search for the description of a godly person because these things do not make a person godly in and of themselves.

In Ephesians 4:1-3 we find some insights into what makes a godly person. "I . . . beseech you to have a walk worthy of the calling with which you were called, with all lowliness and gentleness, with longsuffering, bearing with one another in love, endeavoring to keep the unity of the Spirit in the bond of peace." And later in the same chapter we read, "Let all bitterness, wrath, anger, clamor, and evil speaking be put away from you, with all malice. And be kind to one another, tenderhearted, forgiving one another, just as God in Christ also forgave you" (Ephesians 4:31-32).

"Set your mind on things above, not on things on the earth . . . do not lie one to another . . . put on tender mercies, kindness, humility, meekness, longsuffering; bearing with one another,

and forgiving one another . . . but above all these things put on love . . . and let the peace of God rule in your hearts . . . and be thankful . . . and let the Word of Christ dwell in you richly" (**Colossians 3:2, 9, 12-16**).

If these were the only guidelines we found in God's Word about being a "godly person," we wouldn't lack for information! But there is much more within the pages of Scripture on this topic. It would be a helpful exercise to look for additional verses that bring clarity to the definition of a godly person – according to God's Word. Looking at another source, The International Standard Bible Encyclopedia defines a godly person as "a person who is self-disciplined in godly attitudes and habits!"

The only way we can be self-disciplined in godly attitudes and habits is to learn about God, His Word, and His universal church through biblical education and training. A godly person is one who takes the truth of God's Word and consistently lives it out day-by-day, from the heart, being careful to obey it.

AN ANALOGY

You're sitting in church, listening to a sermon on Luke 7. In the middle of this chapter, you hear a story about a funeral procession wherein a widow is burying her only son. The preacher reminds you that in Jewish culture this woman is in the most despairing situation because if you are a widow and you have lost your only son, this means you have no males to protect or support you. You further learn that this is why a great company from the town is with her. You hear that Jesus walks up to this woman and says, "Don't cry." Your intellect is spurred a little bit; you're stimulated intellectually by all of these little facts. You conclude: "I've learned something new. I've been fed. Therefore, I'm spiritual!" No way. You've just learned some biblical facts that have stimulated you intellectually.

And then consider Jesus' words to the widow, "Don't cry." And you think, in tough times I don't have to cry because Christ is with me and will take care of things. You say, "I've made an application and drafted the application. Therefore, I'm spiritual!" Nope. You've simply made a logical deduction. So you continue to forge an opinion, "When times get tough I will trust Christ. Great—I've more than applied this truth. I have prepared myself for the reaction I should have. Therefore, I'm spiritual!" No, again. You have simply added another "go to" reaction on the flow chart of your mind.

Here is the proper application. When times are tough, you trust Him. And then you run into another tough time, and you trust Him. And yet another tough time comes, and you still proclaim, "I have seen the goodness of God, and I will continue to trust Him. I know He is always with me. He is good and kind and loving and merciful and compassionate and has never winked at my plight; He has never slumbered at my request. I will and I must trust Him again and again – no matter how difficult life becomes." That is the committed faith of a person who is self-disciplined in godly attitudes and habits.

You may be like me. When tough times come, there's an inner battle. Tough times come and you struggle within yourself and think, "Why am I struggling like this?" A truly godly person is someone who is self-disciplined, whose default reaction says, "I will follow God's way, no matter what."

> **"I WILL AND I MUST TRUST HIM AGAIN AND AGAIN – NO MATTER HOW DIFFICULT LIFE BECOMES."**

Allow me to share a personal note. Let me tell you what I do when the Evil One comes with his temptations. I know my flesh well enough to know that I cannot battle against these temptations by myself. My flesh needs an insertion of truth that cuts through my own faulty logic and limitations. So when I face temptation or I struggle spiritually, I often say aloud, "God's way – God's way – God's way!" And as I'm saying this, I slowly begin to see through new eyes. I have learned that our flesh will not want to pursue righteousness. Therefore, we must defeat the cravings of sin before they take root within us. And so in my own weakness, I call out to my Lord by claiming "God's way" over and over. In so doing, I disrupt the flow of the flesh. This is my personal act of self-discipline, as I call on God to help me avoid temptation. A two-fold way to becoming a godly person is: (1) recognize your weakness amid temptation (2) call on God, maybe even verbally, when you are struggling with temptation, or discouragement, or disbelief. I pray you always live life God's way – God's way – God's way!

A LOOK AT YOUR OWN HEART – PSALM 139

I think it is vitally important that we take critical looks at our own hearts from time to time. My favorite Psalm is chapter 139, which I believe is the most beautiful of Psalms. It provides guidance in the examination of our hearts. Verses 1-6 read: "O Lord, You have searched me and known me. You know my sitting down and my rising up; You understand my thought afar off. You comprehend my path and my lying down, and are acquainted with all my ways. For there is not a word on my tongue, but behold, O Lord, You know it altogether. You have hedged me behind and before, and laid Your hand upon me. Such knowledge is too wonderful for me; it is high, I cannot attain it."

Verse 1—*You've searched me and known me*
Verse 2—*You know my sitting down, You understand my thought*
Verse 3—*You comprehend my path, You are acquainted with all my ways*
Verse 4—*There is not a word on my tongue, but Lord, You know it altogether.*
Verse 6—*Such knowledge is too wonderful for me.*

Then in verses 7-12, David speaks of God's omnipresence. He says, "*Where can I go from Your spirit? Or where can I flee from Your presence?*"

Verse 8—*If I make my bed in hell, behold, You are there.*
Verse 9—*If I take (and listen to the Jewish mindset here, the figurative language) the wings of the morning (as quick as the morning creeps up on us), and dwell (or I shoot) in the uttermost parts of the sea, even there Your hand shall lead me, and Your right hand shall hold me.*

In the geography of the Jewish nation of Jerusalem, the sun rises in the east and to their west is the Mediterranean Sea. So to say as quick as the wings of the morning comes (east), and I shoot in the farthest corner of the sea (west), even there Your hand leads me and Your right hand will hold me.

> Verse 11—*If I say, 'Surely the darkness shall fall on me, even the night shall be light about me;*
> Verse 12—*Indeed, the darkness shall not hide from You, but the night shines as the day; The darkness and the light are both alike to You.*

Not being able to hide from God shouldn't be a scary thing. The fact that God knows you through and through should be reassuring to you. I remember in elementary school, if I had a bad report card I was fearful. But bringing home a positive report card for my parents was exciting. Likewise, if our lives are holy, we welcome God fully knowing us. Conversely, if our life has sin in it, then, it's a scary thing. Like John says, "God is light and in Him is no darkness at all" (1 John 1:5). A godly person begs to be transparent and loves God's scrutiny. Your spiritual stability is in direct proportion to how you view God.

> **"LIKEWISE, IF OUR LIVES ARE HOLY, WE WELCOME GOD FULLY KNOWING US."**

Verses 13-16 talk about God's omnipotence; the fact that God is all powerful.

> Verse 13—*For You have formed my inward parts; You have covered me (or knitted me together) in my mother's womb.*
> Verse 14—*I will praise You, for I am fearfully and wonderfully made; Marvelous are Your works, and that my soul knows very well.*
> Verse 15—*My frame was not hidden from You, when I was made in secret, and skillfully wrought in the lowest parts of the earth.*
> Verse 16—*Your eyes saw my substance, being yet unformed. And in Your book they all were written, the days fashioned for me, when as yet there were none of them.*
> Verse 17—*How precious also are Your thoughts to me, O God!*

How great is the sum of them!
Verse 18—*If I should count them, they would be more in number than the sand. When I awake, I am still with You.*
Verse 19—*Oh, that You would slay the wicked, O God! Depart from Me, therefore, you bloodthirsty men.*
Verse 20—*For they speak against You wickedly; Your enemies take Your name in vain.*
Verse 21—*Do I not hate them, O Lord, who hate You? And do I not loathe those who rise up against You?*
Verse 22—*I hate them with perfect hatred; I count them my enemies."*

You think, "Whoa, that's not a psalm of love!" It is important to see that David is saying, "You are a great God that knows all and is everywhere and is so powerful. Your thoughts of us are numerous, even more than the granules of sand on the beach." And David continues, "I love You, and it grieves me when people don't love You like I do." He's literally saying, "Please, as You look upon me, see me differently than You do those who blaspheme You. I don't want anything to do with those who blaspheme You. I don't want to be in their company."

Psalm 1:1-2 says, "Blessed is the man who walks not in the counsel of the ungodly, nor stands in the path of sinners, nor sits in the seat of the scornful; but his delight is in the law of the Lord, and in His law he meditates day and night." I don't want anything in my life that will align me with such people, and I want to separate everything I do from those that blaspheme God. I want to protect my Christian reputation.

Then Psalm 139 ends with, "Search me, O God, and know my heart; try me, and know my anxieties; And see if there is any wicked way in me, and lead me in the way everlasting" (Psalm 139:23-24).

A WILLING SUBMISSION TO HIS WAYS

In Psalm 139:1, David makes the statement, "Lord, You have searched me and known me." Why in the world, if God has searched him and has known him in verse 1, does David then ask God to please search him and know his heart in verse 23 Hasn't God already done this? Doesn't that seem somewhat odd? This is the sign of a strong spiritual man because David is expressing a willing submission to God's ways – all the time. He is saying, "God, I know You already do this, but I want to show You that I'm going to go with You willingly, and I welcome You to search my heart."

When police officers come to the point where they have to take an individual into custody, they ask, "Are you going to cooperate with us or do we have to take you by force?" This is the same concept. God searches us. He knows us, but He wants us to cooperate with Him with a heart that says, "You are a good God; You know me, and I want to know You" (Philippians 3:10, paraphrased). We must welcome His presence and His searching of our hearts. I want to know God and I want to say to Him, "I'm going to go with You everywhere." That is the heart that is willing and open to Christ.

I ask myself, "Am I a godly person?" The answer lies in these two questions: Am I willing to go God's way? Am I willing to open my heart to Him at all times? In light of these same questions, are you a godly person?

HOW IMPORTANT IS MY RELATIONSHIP TO JESUS?

If we love righteousness we will pursue it. If we find joy in the study of God's Word and the life change it brings in our hearts, we will crave righteousness. It's the things that we do grudgingly that will not, after a while, be true of us. For instance, to most men, shopping is an exhausting chore, but for their wives, it brings great joy. The typical man will sit while his wife tries on clothes, and he's almost lazy-eyed he's so tired. But when one of his buddies calls, he's suddenly re-energized when he hears, "Hey, you want to come over and watch ESPN and order some pizza?" He replies, "Yeah! I'll be right over." His wife observes the magical change of attitude and says, "I thought you were tired and wanted to go home." "Well I just got a burst of energy," the husband says sheepishly. We will do what we love to do. This is a picture of our heart with God many times. If our relationship to Jesus is something we value, we'll pursue God's way. That is the heart of a godly Christian.

John 14:1-3 is one of the last words that Jesus shared before making His way to the Garden of Gethsemane prior to His crucifixion. He said, "Let not your heart be troubled; you believe in God, believe also in Me. In

My Father's house are many mansions; if it were not so, I would have told you. I go to prepare a place for you. And if I go and prepare a place for you, I will come again and receive you to Myself; that where I am, there you may be also."

You may ask, how does this have anything to do with how important my relationship is with Jesus? In John 13, the disciples are in the upper room having the last Passover meal, and Jesus is telling them that one of them will betray Him soon. It is unthinkable to the other eleven. And they respond, "Is it me?" None of them say, "Is it Judas?" You see, he had disguised himself so well among them, they never suspected that it would be him. Then Jesus dipped in the sop and turned to Judas, saying, "What you do, do quickly" (John 13:27). Judas left, with the others believing he was getting food for the Passover. Then Jesus turns to His disciples and shares these encouraging words, "Let not your heart be troubled; you believe in God, believe also in Me." (John 14:1). Jesus is telling His disciples that He is credible, considerate, and compassionate. Further, He gives them a little character sketch and reminds them of how much He loves them.

Just like we read in Psalm 139, using the same words to describe His character, Jesus conveys to His disciples what He needs to see in their character. In essence, Jesus was telling them, "I need to see faithfulness from you. If you committed your heart to Me, I need you to be faithful."

Jesus then draws an analogy to a Jewish marriage ceremony, literally describing how a man gets engaged. You see, if a Jewish man wanted to be engaged, he would take his dad and the woman to visit the woman's dad. The young man would turn to the woman's father and say, "I want to marry your daughter." And the father would answer, "Fine, but it will cost you." And then they negotiated all that the groom-to-be would have to provide for the bride. It was called "a bride price." The young man would agree to work a certain amount of years, give his father-in-law livestock, and promise him certain possessions. In fact, the bride price would rival the price of a middle-class home.

The father of the bride would finally stop negotiations when he agreed

> "IF OUR RELATIONSHIP TO JESUS IS SOMETHING WE VALUE, WE'LL PURSUE GOD'S WAY. THAT IS THE HEART OF A GODLY CHRISTIAN. "

that the bride price was sufficient. Then the father-in-law took a cup of wine, and he put it to his lips stating that he accepted the bride price if the groom chose to pay it. He would then give the cup of wine to the groom, and if the groom put it to his lips that signified that he agreed to pay the bride price. Then the groom would turn to the young woman and extend the cup toward her and say, "This is the cup of my new covenant; will you drink?" The future bride had two options: (1) reject the cup (2) put it to her lips, indicating that she was accepting the bride price. If she chose option 2, the couple was espoused, immediately. It would take a write of divorce to break this bond. Interestingly, they would have a very small meal together at this time and not a big ceremony.

Afterward, the young man and his family would bid the bride and her family farewell and leave for a period of about twelve months. Back at his father's home, the young man immediately began renovations to prepare for his bride to come live there. During this same period, she has ceased all of her responsibilities. Along with her mother and other married women, she concentrated her whole heart and mind on her future married life with her soon-to-be husband. She studied different portions of writings and teachings in order to learn how to be a godly woman.

After twelve months passed, the groom dressed in white and made the trek back to the bride's home. As the young man approached, from rooftop to rooftop people would shout, "He's coming! He's coming!" As the young man arrived at her door, the shouts continued, "He's coming!" She was dressed in white, waiting with her bridesmaids. He stood away from the door, and when he blew the shofar horn, she came out the door to greet him. He took her by the hand and together they went back to his father's house where they celebrated with a seven-day festival, a tradition wherein she was veiled. According to this tradition, after the seventh day, her veil was raised so everyone could see who the bride was.

It was essential to explain the Jewish engagement tradition because in the middle of the Passover meal with His disciples, Jesus uses this tradition as an analogy to calm their anxious hearts. Jesus says, "Let not your heart be troubled . . . . ." He was essentially saying, "I'm leaving, but I'm coming back for you as a groom who returns for his bride. Know that

My heart, My mind, and My thoughts are on you. I love you; how precious are My thoughts unto you."

APPLICATION

Today, we stand right where the bride and disciples stood. And Jesus is saying to us, "While I'm gone, be faithful to Me." In fact, in the Jewish culture, if the bride was unfaithful during that year, the man would have to divorce her. It was not an option to remain engaged. That was the situation that Mary and Joseph were in when Joseph heard that Mary was with child. He was going to divorce her privately, but the angel interrupted and said, "No, it's the Holy Spirit who is the Father." Today, we are standing as the waiting bride – preparing our entire minds, our hearts, and our lives for "married life" with Him.

I think of 2 Corinthians 11:2-3, "For I am jealous for you with godly jealousy. For I have betrothed you to one husband that I may present you as a chaste virgin to Christ. But I fear, lest somehow, as the serpent deceived Eve by his craftiness, so your minds may be corrupted from the simplicity that is in Christ."

In other words, some of us cheat on our Husband, Jesus. Where are you? How valuable is your relationship with Him? Is it precious enough that you are a self-disciplined person with godly attitudes and habits. Every time we take the cup of communion, we remember not only the blood of Christ that was shed for us and His body that was broken for us, but we also remember the new covenant. Paul said in 1 Corinthians 11:25, "This cup is the new covenant." Jesus stood at the last Passover meal, and said, "This cup is the new covenant" (Luke 22:20). He reminds us that we have committed our lives to Him.

And so we see that before we can talk about evangelizing, we must first talk about our own hearts and how we represent God to the world.

WRITE IT DOWN:

Are you a godly person according to the biblical definition? Is your "default reaction" one of obedience to the Holy One? How does this relate to the way you serve others?

How are you preparing for "married life" with Jesus according to the analogy used in John 14?

NOTES

SEVEN

Share With Others

CHAPTER SEVEN: *Share With Others*

Nothing will instill a doctrine, life-lesson, principle, or skill into a person's mind more than having to teach it to someone else. Teaching forces a person to not only study a particular topic so they comprehend it, but also to study the material with the goal to clearly present it so others can understand it as well.

The same is true in the development of our spiritual lives. Spending time reading the Bible and other writings is indeed a great start, but a person can better instill in themselves biblical truths by also teaching or sharing these truths with others. This chapter will give you suggestions as to how you can practically share with others the same truths that you are currently learning.

The manner in which we present the gospel may vary depending on the audience. However, the message must remain the same. For instance, the way I present the gospel to a child would be different from the way I would present the gospel to an unsaved adult. Yet, I want to caution us that we must be careful never to compromise the truth for the sake of the audience. We cannot skew any fact of the gospel, or leave out any detail regardless of the individual, environment, or scenario.

> **"... WE MUST BE CAREFUL NEVER TO COMPROMISE THE TRUTH FOR THE SAKE OF THE AUDIENCE."**

With my biblical studies students, I encourage them to learn how to convert theological definitions into language a four-year-old could comprehend. One stipulation is that they cannot cut corners on the truth. I assign them a word like *sanctification* and give them fifteen minutes to discuss it amongst themselves. Then I ask them to demonstrate how they would explain the concept of sanctification to a four-year-old.

Another group is assigned the word *heart*. I tell them the heart is the center and seat of our emotions, the very decision force within us. The heart is the center of our will. Then I ask them to demonstrate how they would explain these ideas to a four-year-old. The mind of a child and their innocence is fascinating. A pastor once told me a story about a man in his congregation who had a heart transplant. When a child heard about the heart transplant, she asked the man if he needed to ask Jesus into his heart again. Of course we think that's sweet; we can picture a child saying that because they think in literal terms. Obviously, there's a deeper meaning. When we use the phrase, "ask Jesus into our heart," we are asking Him to infuse that decision into our heart, into the center and seat of our emotion and intellect, into our very being.

Unfortunately, I believe in our current society some are more interested in the presentation than with the truth of what is being presented. All throughout
the Gospels, Jesus Himself was very cognizant of how He presented truth to individuals. He too seemed to feel that presentation was important. For example, in talking about giving alms, He brought up nuances about the theater. He says (paraphrased), "Your right hand shouldn't know what your left hand is doing, but you guys would rather parade around and blow trumpets as you give your alms"(Matthew 6:2-4). And that's a picture of the theater. Key actors would walk through the main road of the city to the theater, and they would applaud and blow trumpets. That was the way Jesus related to them. I think the presentation is very important. I am all about being creative. In fact, the more creative tools to attract the listener the better. However, the ultimate goal is to preach the unadulterated gospel, so I just want to briefly talk about the manner in which we convey these truths.

BE READY

The manner in which we present the truths of the biblical teaching of salvation is definitely addressed in Scripture, and I think it is very important to highlight these verses concerning how we should share the gospel. I want you to view these few verses as different tools in a tool belt. If you are anything like me, I call my father or friends to help me with odd jobs because I am not a handy man, by any means. These guys all have well-equipped tool belts. When they approach a certain job, they grab the right tool and get to work. They don't waste time running to the other side of the house to grab another tool. All of their tools are "on the ready."

I think it would be a little ridiculous if we hired a handy man that only had one tool on his tool belt, and he used that one tool for every single job. Likewise, I want you to look at these different methods of sharing the gospel as different tools. There may be an occasion where you are more forceful, but then there may be times where you can simply converse with a person. Let's take a look at a few methods.

1 Peter 3:15 says, "But in your hearts set apart Christ as Lord. Always be prepared to give an answer . . ." (NIV). It's this *word* answer that is really interesting. There are many ways to give answers. You can respond militarily, competitively, angrily, or passively. In Scripture there are different ways to give an answer as well. In the book of Colossians, Paul answers back some opponents polemically, which literally means to wage war. You can understand why he would do that because they claimed that Jesus Christ was not God. Rather, they said that Jesus was a nice angel – and He and every other angel must be worshipped –but they argued that Jesus was not really God; nor was He sufficient for salvation. So Paul is very polemic in Colossians 1:15,18 when he said, "He [Christ] is the image of the invisible God, the firstborn over all creation. For by Him all things were created that are in heaven and that are on earth . . . And He is the head of the body, the church . . ." Paul was very specific and very bold in his answer to the Colossians.

In 1 Peter 3:15 the word *answer* is the term that means to give an answer, but it is used in the sense as a lawyer would give an answer in a courtroom. Think about this analogy: The lawyer comes in and has to be cognizant of the judge. There is a jury listening who is less knowledgeable, and he has a formidable foe across the aisle listening to every participle of a sentence and scrutinizing it. He has to remember that he also must give comfort to the one who has entrusted his life to defend him. The lawyer cannot lose his cool; his presentation has to be calm. If he gets dramatic, it is emotional only for effect. He cannot become overly angry, or he will either be in contempt or he will offend the jury with his personality and risk that his anger could cause the jury to overlook the facts. In dealing with the facts, the lawyer has to have them well thought out, with a very systematic approach, and have a very well-rehearsed presentation. He has to know the arguments, points, and counterpoints twelve steps into the process.

Long gone is the response given in the Scopes trials, "God said it, I believe it, and that settles it." That answer branded Christians as being uneducated. If His Word is truth, it will be able to stand the test of any examination, successfully refuting any scrutiny – so it is fine to put it to the test. God's Word is much like an anvil. Many things are pounded upon it and tools may wear down, yet the anvil stands. That's the Word of God. So be systematic, be thoughtful, be well-prepared and be ready to give answers. Incidentally, I have found that preparation breeds confidence. It is healthy to be well-prepared and ready to field arguments and questions, and it is wise to know what principles guide your answers.

REASON WITH THEM

Paul reasoned with them and asked people to reason with him. I think it's important to know that God is very aware of our life and our circumstances. In 1 Corinthians it says that Apollos watered and Paul preached, and they were considered to be equals in ministry. I think we ought to all share the gospel to bring a person to a decision, yet if they don't come to a decision immediately, ask them to consider the gospel again. It's okay after you've sensed a hesitation to ask them to reason and think it over. You do not want to stir their emotions for the sole purpose of getting the response you're looking for. Believe me, they may be emotionally stirred, but you do not want to stir their emotions just to hear them say the desired words. Rather, you want their heart to be changed. There are some individuals that need time to process all the truth you have just presented. Give the seed of truth time to take root.

"IT'S OKAY AFTER YOU'VE SENSED A HESITATION TO ASK THEM TO REASON AND THINK IT OVER."

HAVE RESTRAINT

Another passage that is often overlooked is 1 Corinthians 1:18. It talks about having restraint and not quickly being offended. "For the message of the cross is foolishness to those who are perishing, but to us who are being saved it is the power of God." In other words, when you talk to someone about the gospel, you have to approach the conversation with a level of restraint. Even though you know the precious truth and understand the glorious gospel, the most intelligent unbeliever cannot fully comprehend the preciousness of the gospel until the moment they are convicted to accept Christ. They can watch the movie "The Passion" and be stirred, but those who are unbelievers can never really know the precious treasure they are treading on. In Matthew 7:6 it says, "Do not . . . cast your pearls before swine, lest they trample them under their feet . . ." Literally, it is this precious jewel these animals do not even understand. They are pushing the pearls around with their noses and stomping on them with their feet. They do not really understand what they are treading on at all. If you are evangelizing an unbeliever, they will not know what blasphemy they are uttering. According to Ephesians 2:1-3, their entire conduct is offensive to God.

Paul even regretted some of the words he himself uttered about Jesus Christ. In 1 Timothy 1:12-16 he says, "And I thank Christ Jesus our Lord who has enabled me, because He counted me faithful, putting me into the ministry, although I was formerly a blasphemer, a persecutor, and an insolent man; but I obtained mercy because I did it ignorantly in unbelief. And the grace of our Lord was exceedingly abundant, with faith and love which are in Christ Jesus. This is a faithful saying and worthy of all acceptance, that Christ Jesus came into the world to save sinners, of whom I am chief. However, for this reason I obtained mercy, that in me first Jesus Christ might show all longsuffering, as a pattern to those who are going to believe on Him for everlasting life."

You try to caution this individual, but if you're witnessing don't be surprised if they tread on something blasphemous if they are not a believer. You must have restraint. Unfortunately, they don't know the precious truth upon which they are treading.

BEFRIEND THEM

In 2 John 9-10, we read about how to maintain a standard of limited courtesies toward those who refuse the gospel. These verses speak about sharing the gospel with someone who is hostile to the teachings of the gospel. How do you know when it is time to stop talking to those who have rejected the gospel time and time again? My advice is this: When you have said all that you can say, they know the script, they know everything you are going say, and they still remain hostile – then, you have done your part. Continue to pray for them, and begin sharing with others whose hearts are ready to receive the truth. Of course, if they still have honest questions, then continue the discussion and ask the Lord to direct your conversations.

Matthew 10:14 speaks to those who are hostile to the truth; not to those sincerely seeking, "And whoever will not receive you nor hear your words, when you depart from that house or city, shake off the dust from your feet. Likewise, Luke gives the following account in Acts 13:50-51, "But the Jews stirred up the devout and prominent women and the chief men of the city, raised up persecution against Paul and Barnabas, and expelled them from their region. But they shook off the dust from their feet against them, and came to Iconium."

Also notice another verse that addresses the same concept. It says not to bid them "godspeed" (2 John 10, KJV). This term means that you should not extend to hostile unbelievers the small and seemingly insignificant accolades that we often extend to other believers. For example, I will personally end an email to a believer with a phrase like "God Bless," then type my name. But when I know that I am emailing an unbeliever, I will politely conclude the email with "Sincerely" or "Hope you have a great day." To share meaningful spiritual encouragements with unbelievers may very well make them content with how they are spiritually – all the while they remain lost and in their sinful state. Until they accept what you share, there is still a distinction between all who are saved and those who are lost (2 John 9-10).

TAKE TIME TO LISTEN

It is so important that we take time to rehearse what the specific and necessary biblical truths are so that we are biblically accurate. But we must also take time with the same level of scrutiny to assess and listen to the life situation of the person with whom we are sharing the gospel. Then we can better measure what words will minister most effectively to the heart of the one receiving the message. After rehearsing all of these

"IT IS SO IMPORTANT THAT WE ... ARE BIBLICALLY ACCURATE."

biblical principles related to tact, people skills and the means by which to share these principles, I am reminded of the time tested, universal teachings that the Bible provides for you and me that encourage us to be mindful of the life story of those we meet. For example, Colossians 4:5 comes to mind where it encourages us to "Walk in wisdom toward those who are outside, redeeming the time." Another verse that encourages us to use various approaches for different personalities is 1 Thessalonians 5:14, "Now we exhort you, brethren, warn those who are unruly, comfort the fainthearted, uphold the weak, be patient with all."

Think about all the people in your life who have carefully framed their words to help you understand a concept, the error of your ways, or have given a soft correction or tender rebuke. And they have done it in such a way that their thoughtfulness and consideration left your heart encouraged instead of crushed! They helped turn what could have been a horrible, painful memory into a time of learning, growing, and thankfulness. We are blessed to have these people in our lives, and we can be a blessing in return as we remember to present the biggest love story to the world in the same spirit.

"AND THEY HAVE DONE IT IN SUCH A WAY THAT THEIR THOUGHTFULNESS AND CONSIDERATION LEFT YOUR HEART ENCOURAGED INSTEAD OF CRUSHED!"

WRITE IT DOWN:

Recall the last time you shared the message of salvation with someone. Were you ready? What were some questions that they asked you that you could have answered better if you had been more prepared? How did the conversation end?

Take some time to think about those you know who are in need of salvation.

Who are they? Write down their names. Pray for them. What can you do to move your relationship into one that welcomes sharing the gospel?

NOTES

CONCLUSION

The Call

We have spent some time discussing how to enter into an intimate relationship with Jesus Christ, how to cultivate and maintain that intimacy throughout our lives, and how to share the wonderful story of His grace and love with others. But I would be remiss if I didn't share one final thought with you in order to round out this entire spiritual discussion. I need to answer the question, "So, how do I practically live out all of these principles in my day-to-day life?"

I would consider this book incomplete if I didn't take the time to provide some very practical recommendations for living out these principles on a daily basis. Without the addition of these recommendations, it would be like a lecture that fails to explain how the teachings of the discipline can be integrated into the real world. Or like a pastor, who after he elucidates the most acute, profound points of a theological doctrine, fails to show how that very truth is able to affect the daily lives of the parishioner.

Here are some practical suggestions on how you can live out the spiritual teachings found in this book. Practice them regularly. Remain sensitive to the Holy Spirit's guidance on how to pray during your practice of these spiritual activities. And be careful never to forget that you need to be performing these activities with your whole heart, not simply mechanically checking them off your list.

KNOW

Try solidifying the teachings in chapters one and two in your mind by asking a believing friend to pose some questions – as if he or she is an unbeliever who is sincerely seeking to know what the Bible says about the truth of salvation in Jesus Christ.

Here are some questions you should be prepared to answer:

1. *Why do I need to be saved?*
2. *Is everyone in need of salvation?*

3. *Can I save myself?*

4. *Can I approach God assuming that He will give me—a nice, respectful Person—a "pass" and not hold me to the same level of spiritual scrutiny that He holds other people to?*

5. *What is God's role in saving my soul?*

6. *Is everyone automatically saved since Jesus died and rose again?*

7. *Is having a cognitive knowledge of all the truths presented in chapter one enough to be saved?*

8. *What is the difference between "cognitive" knowledge and "volitional" knowledge of these saving truths?*

9. *Create your own additional questions that you believe would help you retain and comprehend all the teachings in these chapters.*

And be prepared for one more thing. After one of these initial questions, assume that your friend will follow up with this question, "How do you know that?" This will require that you thoroughly understand the Bible references that you quote to your friend when responding to the initial questions.

Now, turn the tables and you play the role of the inquiring unbeliever and have your friend respond to these questions. You may think that your friend has it easier because he/she just heard your response, but this is not always the case. Knowing the concept and hearing the concept audibly is one thing, but clearly verbalizing the concept to a friend in a concise fashion is very challenging.

When you understand the teachings fairly well, you ought to prepare a mini salvation presentation. For example, pretend that you are walking in a parking lot and meet a friend, coworker, or colleague. You find yourself walking together into the building. You both walk through the lobby and approach the elevator. Right as you enter the elevator, your colleague, knowing you are a Christian, asks you, "Hey, could you tell me what it means to be saved?" In this scenario, you have twelve floors and approximately 45-60 seconds to share the gospel – as long as no one else gets on the elevator for those twelve floors. This is indeed the ideal time to share your previously prepared, mini salvation presentation.

Here are some suggestions:

1. Write out the essential elements that absolutely must be communicated concerning salvation.

2. Decide what can be discussed in a follow-up conversation. That is, determine what details are not essential to the initial salvation presentation. You don't want to get too far ahead of yourself and confuse the issue.

3. Rehearse this presentation with a friend. The goal is to have a well-prepared, well-thought-out, sincere presentation.

4. Go out with a friend and look for 45-60 second opportunities. I know that may sound strange but remember, in today's society, time is precious, and people are not normally going to make a major decision in 45-60 seconds. Look at this as a first step in the witnessing process. Others will water the seed you have planted, and God will bring the increase. Who knows, 45 seconds may turn into 45 minutes, and God may provide you with the incredible blessing of seeing a spiritual miracle occur right in front of your eyes!

5. Now, for the biggest challenge. Convert this 45-60 second presentation into the language of a four-year-old without skewing or omitting any truth. Be vivid, imaginative, patient, and very prepared. Consider it a victory if they are able to grasp only one piece of the salvation puzzle during your conversation. Rehearse this a few times introducing new information each time until it becomes natural, and you are at ease with it. God will use it to illuminate the mind by the work of the Spirit in another person's soul.

As a lecturer, I have never understood why we adults have made instructional times so boring. I think you will find that a child-like presentation works well for adults when it comes to the salvation message.

In addition to these activities, go back and rehearse your own personal thoughts and reflections that you wrote down in the "Write It Down" section at the end of Chapter Two. As the apostle John encourages us in Revelation 2:5, "Remember, therefore, from where you have fallen . . . ." It is good to dwell, not on the sin and damage done, but on the miraculous delivery God has provided in our lives. And there is no greater deliverance than that of God's salvation of our souls.

DO JUSTLY

So, how did you do going through the spiritual simulator presented in Psalm 46? Did you pass the test? Do you think you could you trust God as you imagined all of these life-altering circumstances happening to you? Sure, you can reset the simulator even if you didn't pass the test, but in real life it is not that simple.

The first and most important way to begin to live and "*Do Justly*" is to trust the Lord in each and every circumstance of life. And one of the most necessary spiritual disciplines that a believer can cultivate is the commitment to trust God and remain faithful to Him *prior to* experiencing the deliverance of God. While we know that God will calm the raging sea of trouble, doubt, fear, and anxiety in our lives, we must trust Him *prior* to experiencing His promised delivery.

In addition, if the Bible is crystal clear on how we should live, then why don't we obey what the Bible teaches us? I believe that the reason why people do not obey the well-defined biblical instructions is because they *choose* not to obey. How is your commitment to obeying God as your default reaction in your circumstances? And most importantly, are you living out your faith in society? Consider asking a close believing friend to join you in an intentional spiritual discussion about where you are in your spiritual life. Based on your conversation, develop a spiritual plan to practice righteousness on a daily basis, and join together in scheduled prayer times to further develop the spiritual disciplines of trust and obedience.

So the question for you and me is simple, "Will you trust God *before* you experience His deliverance from your challenging circumstances?"

How strong is your faith at this point in your spiritual walk? What have you done to strengthen your "trust factor?" Have you taken time to talk with another believer and ask for spiritual accountability from him/her? Have you consciously inserted spiritual practices into your life that promote consistent obedience? Or, have you simply asked God to help you become a stronger, more passionate Christian without taking any proactive steps to cultivate positive spiritual growth in your life?

I encourage you to become proactive in doing whatever it takes in your life to build a faith in God that trusts Him *prior* to Him displaying His power over your circumstances. Trusting God in the waiting is probably the most obvious sign of a believer who is truly living to "Do Justly."

LOVE MERCY

Think about how your life would be if you were not granted any level of mercy. Consider how your life would be different today if you had not received mercy from anyone. Take time to fill-in-the blanks in the following sentences:

"Were it not for mercy, (<u>insert the name of a friend</u>) and I would probably not be friends today."

"Were it not for mercy, I would probably not be in the (<u>type of relationship</u>) today."

"Were it not for mercy, I may not have experienced (<u>name an accomplishment</u>) in my life."

"Were it not for mercy, I probably would not be able to enjoy the peaceful fellowship of (<u>name of a loved one</u>)."

"Were it not for mercy, (<u>fill in your name</u>)'s soul would be eternally lost."

I want to encourage you to really take a serious look at how mercy has affected your life. Ask yourself if you have made the same positive

"THINK ABOUT HOW YOUR LIFE WOULD BE IF YOU WERE NOT GRANTED ANY LEVEL OF MERCY."

impact upon someone else's life, or if you are withholding mercy towards someone else.

Take time this week to pray about this particular issue of mercy. Ask God to bring to your heart the names of specific people to whom you should display mercy, and take time to thank those around you who have demonstrated a great level of mercy to you. Make a commitment to thank God daily for His indescribable gift of mercy in providing salvation for your soul.

WALK HUMBLY

As you strive to live a truly humble life before the Lord, I encourage you to always ask the "ME" question before you present a sermon, devotional, Bible study lesson, or offer advice to a friend. This means that, before you present a truth from God's Word, take a moment to pray, "God, I am about to share [this truth] from Your Word. Please help ME be mindful of my own weaknesses. Help ME be the FIRST one to apply the teachings of Your Word. Keep ME sensitive to Your Word."

Do self-examination regularly. Pray the prayer of self-examination that is found in Psalm 139:23-24, *"Search me, O God, and know my heart; Try me, and know my anxieties; And see if there is any wicked way in me, And lead me in the way everlasting."*

"I ENCOURAGE YOU TO ALWAYS ASK THE 'ME' QUESTION."

If, during your self-examination, God answers your prayer and indeed exposes a "wicked way in you," do not allow one more minute to pass before you examine where and when you failed in this area. Then confess your sin to God and tell Him exactly what you are going to do to safeguard from ever falling into that sin again. Be sure that your safeguards include meditating on the Scriptures, and implement these safeguards immediately.

As much as you can this week, be intentional to enter into conversations regarding spiritual issues. Try not to enter into discussions for the purpose

"BE INTENTIONAL TO ENTER INTO CONVERSATIONS REGARDING SPIRITUAL ISSUES."

of debate, but rather for the purpose of hearing how the truths of God are speaking to the hearts of your friends, family, and fellow believers. Simple discussions over basic spiritual issues often produce a desire in the participants' hearts to do it again, and again. For example, you can ask someone: "What characteristic of God do you find most comforting and why?" "What is one thing that you remember from Sunday's sermon (or recent Bible study lesson, devotional, etc.) that the Holy Spirit is causing you to rehearse in your mind over and over this week?" "Was there a time in your life when God demonstrated His power, compassion, or provision to you? And in looking back, have you concluded that there is no way anyone could have orchestrated the situation except God Himself?"

Have your discussion group read this chapter on biblical humility and discuss it in your Bible study groups. Attempt to link the teaching from this chapter to other portions of the Bible that also speak to the importance of cultivating humility in the believer's life.

SERVE OTHERS

This chapter would be great for group discussion. It contains a lot of points that tend to be of interest to many believers. I only wish I could attend some of your discussion groups as you process the spiritual teachings presented in this chapter. Here are some leading questions I encourage you to discuss:

1. How would you answer this question, "What is a godly person?"

2. What was your initial thought when you read that there is a difference between a mere Christian and a godly Christian? Possibly consider Galatians 6:1 where it describes how believers ought to not only keep a fallen believer accountable, but also restore him or her "in a spirit of gentleness."

3. What is your opinion of the definition of a godly person being one who is self-disciplined in godly attitudes and habits?

4. Prayerfully ask everyone in the group if they are indeed a godly person. Have a time of prayer so that your discussion group members can ask the Lord to forgive them and/or thank Him for His power to become a godly person once again.

Read Psalm 139 per the basic outline that I provided in Chapter Six. This time, take time to stop and pause at the end of each section to reflect on the details of God's immutable attributes (omniscience, omnipresence, and omnipotence). Spend one session on each division of this Psalm to ponder the vastness of the greatness of our God. Then take time to comprehend the great care that the Psalmist took to tell God that he wanted to be looked upon as different from anyone who finds it easy to blaspheme the Lord. Ask yourself if you do all you can do to make sure that you are far removed from anything that would cause people to think that you do not honor the Lord Jesus Christ. Think of little things you could do that would make a tactful statement to all that you are indeed different.

Consider the teaching of John 14:1-3 and ask the very simple question, "Am I a faithful bride?" This question could go two ways in your life. I would encourage you to identify what you believe you are doing that the Lord is indeed pleased with. I know this may be somewhat uncomfortable for some because you actually will be articulating things that you believe you are doing right before the Lord. But don't feel that you are being prideful or arrogant. You could preface your statements with these words, "Lord, thank You for giving me the wisdom to see what I need to do. Keep me close to You and I will strive to remain obedient to You." Remember, as a Father, our Lord longs to hear of the obedience of His children, and He longs to bless His children immensely. Also, identify what areas of your life you could improve on so that you are always living as a faithful bride. As you do this, pray to the Lord – the One who both loves you and desires the absolute best for you – and tell Him why you think you have been tempted to disobey Him in specific areas of your life. Confess to Him that you are sorry and that you regret giving in to those passions. Then, begin to tell Him what you will do for the remainder of the day to safeguard your heart and mind from considering being unfaithful to Him.

Don't try to gain spiritual victory in one all-encompassing action or activity. You did not just fall into sin all of a sudden, nor will the recovery back to a strong state require only one magical action or activity. You need to take baby steps in your spiritual walk – one day at a time. Create little and numerous spiritual victories in your life. Take time to praise the Lord and celebrate these times of obedience by talking with a friend and let them know that, "Hey, I made it through another day" or "We had a good time focusing on spiritual things tonight, and my mind was focused more than it has been in a long time."

Make a list or keep a journal of what seem to be "little spiritual victories" that you could celebrate and praise the Lord for. Consider if there are daily victories, half-day victories, even hourly victories. I believe this ability of seeing progress and experiencing victories will encourage you not to throw away all that the Spirit has done and is obviously doing in your life to keep you faithful to Him!

SHARE WITH OTHERS

Building on what we practiced in Chapters One and Two, begin now to prepare for a longer presentation of the gospel lasting 4-7 minutes. Take what you have learned in Chapter Seven and begin to work on a well-framed, systematic, well-thought-out presentation of the gospel. Prepare a presentation for a receptive seeker who is kind, courteous, and willing to listen. Be prepared for questions that may not relate to what you are trying to share. Also be prepared for someone who may have a hostile reaction and wants to argue. Remember, what dispels fear is confidence in God and a well-prepared presentation.

Again, build on what we practiced in Chapters One and Two, rather than have a random encounter with a stranger. Take a moment to think of someone specifically who is in need of hearing the gospel message. Begin praying for this person by name. Tell the Lord how you feel about this person and why you chose his/her name. Tell the Lord how you feel about sharing the gospel with him/her. Are you scared? Nervous? Excited? Impatient? Happy? Sad? Then articulate to God exactly why you feel this way. Rehearse the teachings that you learned in Chapters One, Two, and Seven, and see if these verses provide the knowledge that you need in order to overcome your fears. Of course, Chapters One and Two provide the Bible's teaching on what salvation is and is not. Chapter Seven encourages you to be prepared in many ways as you share these truths with others.

So, the only remaining fear is possibly, "What if they ask me a question that is not addressed in this book?" Then your answer is, "Well, good question. I don't know the answer right now, but if you would allow me a little time, I'll ask someone who may know and/or find a resource that answers your question. Then I'll get back with you." Remember, unless you are a scholar with a Ph.D. in every academic field of discipline, you are bound to say, "I don't know" a few million times in your lifetime. There is no shame in not knowing how to respond immediately.

Simply write down the question, or make a list if they have several questions, and then tell them that you will research the answer and get back to them. But be quick to ask them a question in return, "If I take the time to research the issue, and I return to you with a response that supports the Bible and its teaching about salvation, will you then believe that the Bible is true and give your heart to Jesus Christ?" Of course, if someone is not sincere, they will shrug this off and give other excuses as to why they do not believe – and that shows you that regardless, their heart is set on not believing in Jesus Christ. But the sincere ones will realize that they will be put to a point of decision if you return with sound answers to their questions.

Remember also that when you are witnessing and being kind and respectful as Chapter Seven teaches, you are not the only one who has to answer questions. It is also incumbent upon the one to whom you are witnessing to respond to your questions as well. So ask them a lot of questions. Make them tell you what they believe about salvation. Ask them follow up questions like, "So, according to your way, I could work for my own salvation. So, how do I know when I have done enough good things? Who makes this judgment call? Do other imperfect humans decide this?" Or a line of questioning like, "If peace is found within ourselves, how do I know I am always right and guiding myself down a healthy path? Do I know if my path is perfect until I become perfect and all-knowing? Has anyone ever reached that goal of perfection? If so, should we then begin to consult him/her?"

Ask questions of the ones you are witnessing to and listen to them.

Then after you have asked them questions and listened to them, ask them more questions about their beliefs and listen some more. You may find that the more they rehearse their belief system, the more they realize the gaping holes in it.

"ASK QUESTIONS OF THE ONES YOU ARE WITNESSING TO AND LISTEN TO THEM."

THE CALL

I have heard it said that, "Practice does not make perfect. Practice only makes permanent. Perfect practice makes perfect." The spiritual activities presented in this final chapter are for the purpose of spurring you on to practice what you have learned in this book. Of course, there are many more activities and ideas that would help you solidify these teachings in your heart. So, I encourage you to think of more ways – unique ways – that you believe would honor the Lord, protect the pure gospel message, and be effective in reaching others with the saving knowledge of Jesus Christ. My deepest heart's cry for you as a believer in Jesus Christ is for you to know the Lord more intimately, testify of His saving grace, love, and mercy to those around you, and for you to be a walking example of holiness, righteousness, and purity before those who are observing you and looking up to you for a spiritual example by which to model their own lives.

Life is too short and God's truth too precious to keep His message contained within us or to squander our testimony by pursuing sin. Even though my heart desires to join each and every one of you at your churches, ministries, and missions, and to worship with you in rehearsing these wonderful truths together, my only request is that you make a lifetime commitment to purpose in your heart to live out the following words of the apostle Paul:

"Dear friends, you always followed my instructions when I was with you. And now that I am away, it is even more important. Work hard to show the results of your salvation, obeying God with deep reverence and fear. For God is working in you, giving you the desire and the power to do what pleases him."
(Philippians 2:12-13 NLT)

NOTES

ABOUT THE AUTHOR

Dr. Ben Gutierrez is a Professor of Religion at Liberty University and a member of the Executive Leadership Team at Thomas Road Baptist Church, Lynchburg, Virginia. Dr. Gutierrez received a Diploma from Word of Life Bible Institute, an AA and BS in Religion from Liberty University, a Master of Arts in Religion and a Master of Divinity from Liberty Baptist Theological Seminary, as well as a PhD from Regent University.

He is the co-author of Learn to Read New Testament Greek Workbook (2009) published by Broadman & Holman, an excellent resource to supplement one's study of the Koine Greek language; co-editor of The Essence of the New Testament: A Survey (2012) published by Broadman & Holman, a survey of the New Testament that provides a practical, readable, and insightful survey of theological concepts, practical applications, study questions, and helpful word studies; co-author of Ministry Is: How to Serve Jesus with Passion and Confidence (2010) published by Broadman & Holman, a Bible-based, practical guide to serving God within the local church; and author of Living Out the Mind of Christ - Practical Keys to Discovering and Applying the Mind of Christ in Everyday Life (2011) by Academx — a recommended Innovate Church resource for all pastors and Christian leaders.

Dr. Gutierrez and his wife Tammy have two daughters, Lauren and Emma, and reside in Forest, VA.

NOTES

NOTES

Re·Entry

MAKING THE
TRANSITION
FROM MISSIONS
TO LIFE
AT HOME

Re·Entry

▼▼▼▼▼▼▼▼▼▼▼▼

MAKING THE
TRANSITION
FROM MISSIONS
TO LIFE
AT HOME

Peter Jordan

YWAM
Publishing
A Ministry of Youth With A Mission
P.O. Box 55787, Seattle, WA 98155

YWAM Publishing is the publishing ministry of Youth With A Mission. Youth With A Mission (YWAM) is an international missionary organization of Christians from many denominations dedicated to presenting Jesus Christ to this generation. To this end, YWAM has focused its efforts in three main areas:
1) Training and equipping believers for their part in fulfilling the Great Commission (Matthew 28:19). 2) Personal evangelism. 3) Mercy ministry (medical and relief work).
For a free catalog of books and materials write or call:
YWAM Publishing
P.O. Box 55787, Seattle, WA 98155
(425) 771-1153 or (800) 922-2143
e-mail address: 75701.2772 @ compuserve.com

Re-Entry

Published by Youth With A Mission Publishing
P.O. Box 55787, Seattle, WA 98155, USA.

ISBN 0-927545-40-3

Printed in the United States of America.

Dedication

This book is written for those about to go into missions; for those who currently are in missions; and for those who were in missions, and have experienced the challenges of re-entry....My prayer for some special ones in this last group is that the words and spirit contained herein would bring life and hope and joy back into your hearts. You are the ones who "crashed" and still haven't been able to walk away from the wreckage.

The names and peripheral details concerning some people mentioned in this book have been changed.

Acknowledgments

C.S. Lewis warned, "The yen to publish is spiritually dangerous." The "yen" in this case is spread around, so perhaps the danger is diminished! This book has been "yenned" into existence by many, and is a two-team effort....

Team One is comprised of those who have had major influences for good in my life. Without their touch, even more deficiencies would show. In this team, I include Laurance and Margaret Jordan, who gave me life; Don and Gwen Wilson, who gave me a life partner; Hugh Quigley, Dave Wilson, George Wilkinson, Ernie Tatham, and Eric Johnston, who have been extra fathers to me; Al Weir, Ethel Lee, Keith Price, Joe Kass, Uli and Carol Kortsch, Bruce and Barbara Thompson, David and Dale Garratt, Tom Hallas, and Dan Sneed, who encouraged and exhorted me; Loren Cunningham, who for twelve close-up years showed me what it is to be a man of God; and the one who belongs in both teams—Donna, my wife who has loved me and has prayed for me since at least 1960.

Team Two is made up of those who have helped in the actual writing of this book. God—I trust—initiated it; Donna has constantly breathed encouragement upon it, as has Laurie, my daughter and co-worker, who provided special support at a critical juncture when I was about to pack the whole project in; Ken and Shirley Wright, Chris Galloway, and Wayne and Nancy Jane Johnson have all been advisors and cheerleaders since the beginning; and Geoff and Janet Benge, without whom this book would not have succeeded practically, editorially, or structurally.

My continuing gratitude to all these, and others not mentioned—though they should have been. Jesus knows.

Table of Contents

Foreword

Going on a short-term outreach, or a long-term outreach for that matter, can be like going into outer space. You leave home fast, and you come down hard! And in between is a totally foreign and completely exhilarating experience.

But what happens when you get back home? Will your experience overseas be completely misunderstood by your friends, your local church, and your loved ones? Will you be able to translate the blessings of what you experienced overseas into daily life back home? Will you begin to compare your local church, and the ordinary eight-to-five workday lives of most members, to your exhilarating experience of prayer, evangelism, and close-quarter living with other missionaries and workers?

It is important to ask these questions—and more important to answer them! I believe this book is key in helping every person involved in short-term or long-term missions to come face to face with the key issues of "re-entry." I encourage you to work through these issues, and to commit yourself to redeem everything that God does for you, both in your overseas experience and as you share and apply what you learned back home.

Not only is *Re-Entry* a practical and helpful book for every local church and mission agency who sends workers overseas, but it is fun to read. Peter Jordan shares many anecdotes, metaphors, and insights into aviation and space travel. I loved reading the book, and I know you will, too!

Floyd McClung, Jr.
June, 1992

Happy Landing

As dangerous as it may seem to orbit in a space shuttle 135 miles above the earth at a speed of 18,000 miles per hour, it is relatively risk free. Compared to what? Compared to the risks involved in rocketing the shuttle up into space in the first place, and most certainly compared to the risks involved in bringing it back down to earth. To pass from orbit to terra firma, an astronaut must guide his craft through the turbulent and fiery "re-entry" of the earth's atmosphere, where any wrong maneuver can result in instant incineration.

It is no mistake that the word *re-entry* is also applied to the experience returning missionaries must go through as they make the adjustment from life on the mission field back to life at home. Like the astronaut guiding his craft back into the earth's atmosphere, returning missionaries must negotiate many potential hazards. They too must cover dangerous territory; dangerous in terms of the emotional, spiritual, and relational damage that can occur if the process is not handled correctly. Indeed, if it is not handled correctly, the returning missionary may barely escape with his or her emotional well-being and faith intact.

Can re-entry really be that devastating? What could go wrong? After all, a missionary is returning home to friends and family who love and support him. What could the problem be? I'm sure many astronauts have been tempted to ask such questions as they spin contentedly through space. Everything seems so calm and orderly until the retro rockets are fired and the space shuttle slips out of orbit and begins its descent toward earth.

After we look at the passage through which an astronaut must guide his craft on its way down to earth, we can draw comparisons to the returning missionary's experiences. We'll hitch a ride back to earth aboard the space shuttle *Explorer* as it returns from an eight-day scientific mission in space. Captain Al is our command pilot for this thrilling descent.

Al sits pensively scanning the instruments on the space shuttle's flight deck. He is waiting for the order from ground control to leave orbit. Finally the radio crackles as a voice announces, "*Explorer,* this is Houston. Time to head for home, over."

"Roger, Houston, this is *Explorer.* All systems go." Al punches some information into the shuttle's computer and a pre-programmed sequence of events is set in motion. Tiny forward-facing thrusters are fired for a few moments, long enough to slightly "decay" the space shuttle's orbit, allowing it once again to come under the influence of earth's gravity.

Al braces himself for the ordeal ahead. He has rehearsed the re-entry process many times in a simulator on earth. He must guide *Explorer* down at the right angle so it eases into the earth's atmosphere. If the shuttle enters the earth's atmosphere too rapidly or at too steep an angle, the heat from friction will quickly incinerate it.

As the space shuttle approaches the outer reaches of earth's atmosphere, Al monitors the controls as the craft's speed rapidly decelerates. 18,000 mph...16,500...14,000...11,500...7,000. Now *Explorer* is virtually crawling.

Through the side window, Al can see the fiery plume generated by the heat of re-entry. The rest of the crew see it, as well. Their first reaction is disorientation and fear, but the shuttle is designed to withstand this searing heat, so they relax in the air-conditioned comfort of the shuttle's interior.

Al's eyes methodically scan the instrument panel, monitoring each gauge and switch. The crackle of radio transmissions has died away; the space shuttle is in the "zone of silence." The heat of re-entry has disrupted the flow of radio waves. For five long minutes, Al loses contact with Mission Control. No reassuring words from those on earth who have meticulously fussed over the shuttle's mission since blast-off.

As the space shuttle plunges closer to earth, the fiery heat of re-entry is replaced by the intense cold of the icy reaches of the upper stratosphere. The craft cools quickly, and radio contact with Houston is restored with a crackle. "Welcome back, *Explorer*," the reassuring voice of Mission Control in Houston announces.

As Al reaches across to make some adjustments on his instrument panel, he is suddenly aware that his arms feel like lead. It seems to take so much of his energy to reach out his arm. The wonderful, floating weightlessness of zero gravity that Al and his crew have enjoyed for the last eight days has gone; gravity has kicked back in.

The craft continues to decelerate; 900 mph. Then 750 mph. Now, under manual control, *Explorer* is flying like an airplane. Although Al cannot hear them, behind the craft and on the ground, twin sonic booms sound like double claps of thunder. They announce to those waiting on the ground that *Explorer* has slowed through the sound barrier. The earth looms closer by the moment.

Finally, the beckoning runway of Cape Canaveral is in sight. Al aligns the shuttle for landing, bringing it in over the threshold of the runway at a paltry 250 mph. Twin puffs of smoke indicate that the main wheels are on the ground, and in a few seconds, the craft rolls to a complete stop.

In a few short minutes, Al and his crew have gone from hurtling around the earth at 18,000 mph to standing still. They have descended 135 miles through searing heat and biting cold. They have endured the zone of silence at a time when they most needed the input and reassurance of Mission Control. They have coped with the effects of gravity, and have experienced some disorientation. But they have made it home.

The parallels between this and a missionary leaving the mission field to return home are many. If you are a missionary, you have adjusted to life in another culture, another dimension. In returning home, you must make the adjustment back to the culture and lifestyle you left. What are some of the problem areas to watch for in making the transition?

Heat Build-up

When your period of missions service is complete and you re-enter your home culture, you will find that some heat is generated. The heat can come from outside you, or from within. The external heat will most likely be generated by some of the comments and questions from friends and family who don't really understand what you've been doing. "I bet it was nice out there in Hawaii! How was the surfing?" Or, "It must be great to travel? Did you say the church paid for your vacation?" Or perhaps the heat will come from the fact that no questions are asked or comments made about what you have been doing on the mission field. Apathy and lack of spiritual interest are bitter pills to swallow, especially when you are bursting to tell people about God's faithfulness to you during your absence. Disinterest and indifference generate heat.

On the other hand, internal heat will probably be generated by your inability to fully understand and respond rightly to people who seem to misunderstand you and why you went.

The Zone of Silence

The zone of silence can be a traumatic experience that can last for months, even years. The silence that you encounter as a returning missionary occurs in two areas. First, in leaving the mission field, you are leaving the support structure of friends and co-workers who have guided and nurtured you during your time away. When you arrive home, you must establish a new support structure. Until you do, the silence can be deafening.

Second, if you're not careful, silence can creep into your devotional life. The pressures of re-entry have the unfortunate tendency to push you in the opposite direction to where you want to go. Instead of pushing you closer to God, re-entry stress tends to push you away from Him. A disruption occurs in the flow of your devotional life, and the ensuing silence can be frightening as you try to bear the challenges of re-entry alone.

Gravity Kicks In

While on the mission field, you may have had certain ministry pressures to bear, but they are different pressures to those you will experience at home. At home you will have the demands and expectations of your family, your church, and your culture to deal with. This added "gravity" may manifest itself through feelings of loneliness or periods of depression, anger, or sadness. The only way to deal with this type of "gravity" is to release the weight you are feeling to the Lord, who says, "Come to me, all you who are...burdened....Take my yoke upon you...for my yoke is easy and my burden is light" (Matthew 11:28-30). Unfortunately, as mentioned above, the stress of re-entry often seems to push people in the opposite direction—away from God.

Disorientation Occurs

The dictionary defines *disorientation* as the condition "in which one loses one's perception of time, place or personal identity." Many American astronauts, particularly those who voyaged to the moon and back, reported disorientation following their return. They had been in such a radically different environment that they were no longer sure of their bearings when they returned.

Perhaps you remember hearing about Sergei Krikalev. Sergei is a Russian cosmonaut currently in training for a joint U.S.-Russian space mission. But Sergei's real claim to fame is that he spent 313 days orbiting the earth in the Soviet Mir space station. He wasn't supposed to be up there that long, but his nation, the Soviet Union, was breaking apart below him. People had more important things to worry about than Sergei, so he stayed in space for five months more than the planned length of his mission.

A replacement finally arrived, and Sergei was able to return to earth. When he arrived back on earth, he was woozy, confused, and totally disoriented. Since he had lived in zero gravity for so long, his muscles had atrophied to the point where he was unable to walk.

Re-entry can be a very disorienting time for both astronauts and for returning missionaries, and the longer you have been away, the greater the level of disorientation you are likely to experience.

An "Underwhelming" Welcome Back

When John Glenn, the first American to orbit the earth in a space craft, returned home, he was welcomed as a returning hero. When you mention space travel, his name immediately comes to mind. It was the same for Neil Armstrong, the first man to set foot on the moon.

But ask yourself who the commander of the last space shuttle mission was, and you'll likely draw a blank. Why? Because space travel has become "old hat." Scarcely a month goes by when we don't hear of a space mission. This doesn't lessen the value of what today's space travelers do. The risks are the same, and astronauts today routinely spend more time in space than their pioneering predecessors.

But space travel is no longer new or exciting to the general population. The romance and adventure that people associated with space travel has largely evaporated, so astronauts today are no longer viewed as returning national heroes.

Much the same is true for missions. Hudson Taylor, William Carey, and David Livingston were pioneers in the true sense of the word. But when you return home, don't expect to be treated the way they were. That's not to devalue what you have done and been through; it simply reflects the change in how missionaries are viewed today. Romantic notions of penetrating unexplored regions in search of people to share the Gospel with are few and far between. The majority of missionaries today work in urban settings.

As a missionary just returned from the field, you cannot help but have expectations of how people should treat you. Unfortunately, the reality is that few people are going to live up to your expectations.

———————————

My great desire in writing this book is to help people safely navigate the transition from the mission field to home. As I look back at my own life, I realize that I could have benefited much from the information contained in this book. Of course, when I made my first re-entry to my home culture, there was no space travel metaphor for the experience. Space travel was still something people only dreamed about. Back then, missionaries were simply coming home on furlough.

I was born in China, where my parents were missionaries with Christian Missions in Many Lands. I spent the first eleven years of my life in China, with the last three and a half of those spent in a Japanese concentration camp in Shanghai. After our release from the camp, my family and I boarded a ship for San Francisco. From there, we traveled to Vancouver, then across Canada by train. We finally boarded a troop ship which brought us across the Atlantic to "home"—England—a country I had never before laid eyes on. It was a dreary and dismal place, largely in ruins after the ravages of World War II.

Being home brought feelings of shock and horror. I felt disoriented and lost. I had plenty of family in England, and they all wanted to pat my head, tweak my cheek, and tell me how cute I was. But I felt dreadfully alone. I looked and sounded like a little English boy, but inside I was something else; I didn't know what. In retrospect, I was like an immigrant—or perhaps a refugee—dropped into a strange land. My roots were in China, but I was expected to bloom in England. I never did, and as soon as I graduated from high school at seventeen, I fled to Canada.

Had my parents known what I know today about re-entry, they could have prepared all of us for the experience. But they didn't, and the ignorance with which the transition was approached created great turmoil in my life. My coming-home experience haunted me for years before I was able to finally process it and lay it to rest.

Since then, my wife Donna, our four children, and I have served as missionaries with Youth With A Mission, and in the course of our ministry, have traveled extensively in Asia and the Pacific. From firsthand experience and through talking with many missionaries, we have learned much about the stress of re-entry and how to handle it.

This book is divided into two sections around the space travel metaphor. The first section deals with the practical things that should be attended to before leaving the mission field to lessen the stress. The second section deals with how to handle things once you have arrived home.

As you will see, the book is written with both the long-term and the short-term missionary in mind, though the greater weight of information tends to fall on the side of the short-termer. Short-term missionaries are an important part of today's mission force, but their special needs are often overlooked in literature on the subject of re-entry. However, whether you are a long- or short-term missionary, I trust you find the insights presented in this book helpful and practical.

Happy landing on your re-entry!

Part One:

Preparing to Leave Orbit

1

The Downwind Leg

Most astronauts were pilots first. It's the precision training and discipline of flying that makes a good pilot into a good astronaut. I know, because for a number of years I was a jet pilot for the Royal Canadian Air Force. I know the discipline of practicing landings and takeoffs day in and day out. I've worked to perfect the precision moves necessary for quick maneuver during the heat of battle. Flying is wonderful and exhilarating. It offers the excitement of three-dimensional movement: left/right, up/down, fast/slow, even upside down! But flying can be dangerous. And no part of it is more dangerous than takeoffs and landings.

After a sortie into the wild blue yonder, one thing all pilots agree upon is that "a good landing starts on the downwind leg." What this simply means is that making a really smooooooth landing—pilots call it a "greaser"—starts well before the airplane is lined up into the wind and descending on final approach to the runway. It begins many minutes before touchdown with a careful analysis of the surrounding conditions and preparation for all contingencies.

As a pilot brings his plane down for a landing,

he must fit into the airport traffic pattern. He must also ensure that the aircraft has sufficient fuel, that his airspeed is appropriate, that the wheels are down and the brakes have been tested, and that the flaps are set. All the while, he scans the surrounding airspace to assess what is going on outside the cockpit, keeping a safe distance from other aircraft, and instantly obeying instructions from the control tower. Only then is the pilot ready to set his aircraft down securely upon terra firma.

In the same way, thorough planning is necessary for your return from the mission field. Too many returning missionaries have crashed upon landing, because they mistakenly thought they could glide right back to a smooth touchdown in the culture they left behind. But such crash-landings can be avoided by careful planning.

I like to call this planning *closure*. Closure is the art of bringing to a satisfactory conclusion the passage of life through which we have just passed. Closure enables us to move from one passage of life to another without carrying burdens of guilt and false expectations. It allows us to build on previous experiences instead of camping in the emotional fog of past memories.

This is why some form of funeral service or ritual is important in all cultures. The funeral allows time to honor the one who has passed on, time for the family and spouse to grieve, and a time of farewell to the dead person. Things will never be the same for the family. A transition has occurred. The death of a loved one has taken the family from one passage of life to another.

We can see this process at work in the life of Abraham. Abraham and Sarah enjoyed a long, happy and fulfilling life together. They had made mistakes, but there had also been great blessings. In her old age, Sarah miraculously had become pregnant and had born a son, and God had promised to bless all mankind through that son. Sarah had been Abraham's traveling companion, his source of comfort, his delight, and the love of his life. But at 127 years of age, Sarah died. (The story of her passing is recorded in Genesis 23.)

Abraham mourned and wept for his dead wife. After a time of grieving, he purchased the cave of Machpelah and buried Sarah there. The burial was a transition. Abraham and his son Isaac entered a new passage in their lives. Things would never be the same as they were when Sarah was alive. It didn't mean that God was no longer going to bless or use Abraham, it just meant that He was going to do it differently. Indeed, God had new blessings in store for Abraham. He married again, and his new wife Keturah bore him six more sons (Genesis 25:1-2). Can you imagine remarrying and having six more kids at 130 years of age?

Abraham would never forget Sarah; she would always live in his memories. However, he had mourned for her and then buried her; he had brought closure to that passage of his life. As a result, he was able to make a successful transition into the new blessing that God had in store for him. It wasn't easy for him to bury Sarah, but he recognized that he needed to do it and move on. God was not finished with him yet.

I recently heard a tale about two men who came upon an old woman waiting to cross a river. A storm had swept away the bridge that spanned the river, and the old woman stood pondering her options. As the two men approached her, she recognized them, and asked if they would carry her across. One of the men joyfully agreed to help the old woman; the other man hesitated for a few moments before grudgingly agreeing to assist his companion with the task. The two men stooped down and made a sling with their arms. The old woman sat on their arms, and they ferried her across the river and set her down on the other side.

Several miles down the road, the one man was still complaining about the imposition the old woman had been. "My back hurts from carrying her. Doesn't your back hurt, too? And why are you smiling and singing?" the man asked. Stopping in mid-stride and turning to look at his traveling companion, the other man happily declared, "My back doesn't hurt at all, but that's the difference between you and me—I put the old lady down several miles ago after we crossed the river. You're still carrying her!"

For the last several years, my wife Donna and I have directed camps for returned missionaries. I particularly remember one incident that occurred. At the beginning of one camp, the campers gathered in a large circle to take turns introducing ourselves. Each person told who they were, a little of their background and missionary experience, and something of their current situation.

Everything proceeded in an orderly fashion until it came the turn for one particular man to share. As he tried to speak, he began weeping uncontrollably. Through his tears he sobbed, "I've been back from the mission field for two years, and tonight I feel like I've come home....You are my real family. You understand me. I know I can't go back to the mission field, but I don't seem to belong at home anymore, either." In subsequent camps, and in conversations with many other returned missionaries, I have heard similar sentiments echoed over and over. Like the man in the story who was still "carrying" the old woman, these people were carrying unnecessary burdens.

It is difficult to move successfully into the next passage of your life if you have not brought closure to the preceding passage. Therefore, it is imperative for every returning missionary, be they short-term or long-term, to bring closure to their time on the mission field. Failure to do so means you will never truly leave the mission field behind. It will follow you in your thoughts, in your reactions, and in your future relationships. Like a ghost from the past, it will thwart a positive re-entry experience and will hamper your efforts to adapt to and move into a new passage in your life.

This is not to say you can't have wonderful memories of your time on the mission field. It is simply to say that there should be a closing of the door to that part of your life as you move on; you can't live there any longer. You must live in the present, not in the past.

There are a number of steps you can take to ensure that you bring proper closure to your mission experience. This first section, Leaving Orbit, examines these steps.

The Process of Closure

The first step in the closure process has to do with recognizing and coming to terms with the reasons you are leaving the mission field to return home. For some, this is simple and straightforward. You may be leaving for an extended time of furlough. Or you may have been on a short-term mission project (anything up to two years) which has been completed. Some of you may have made

a longer-term commitment to missions, and your
period of commitment has come to an end. And
still others of you may be aware that God has
specifically called you to some new area of service,
and you are leaving in obedience to His call.

Yet there are those of you for whom it is more
difficult. Your desire is to stay on the mission field,
but circumstances dictate otherwise. For some,
sickness in yourself or in a family member has
caused you to leave the mission field. For others,
your lack of financial resources prohibits you from
staying longer. And for some, it may be difficulty
in obtaining necessary visa extensions, or the
need to return home for your children's education.

In these circumstances, it is easy to feel forced
off the mission field, and such a feeling can easily
lead to disappointment, frustration, bitterness, or
even resentment against God or the mission
agency. When such feelings arise, they must be
dealt with. Left unchecked, such feelings will soon
sap your spirit of energy and vitality, and will send
you into a tailspin.

Every returning missionary should come to the
place where regardless of the circumstance, he
recognizes his return as God's will for him, and
God's way of leading him into a new passage in his
life.

The apostle Paul is a wonderful example of this.
He endured all manner of misfortunes, and saw
each of them as God's new opportunity for spiritual growth and effectiveness. Consider Paul on
his way to Rome to appear before Caesar. For
fourteen days, his ship was buffeted about the
Adriatic Sea by a storm. The vessel finally ran
aground on a shoal off the island of Malta, and
Paul and the ship's crew escaped with their lives

and little else. Malta was still a long way from Rome, but Paul saw it as God's sovereign guiding, and set about to minister the Gospel. For three months, he powerfully introduced the Gospel to the people of Malta.

Amazingly, despite all he endured as he diligently sought to serve the Lord Jesus, Paul summed things up this way: "We know that in *all* things God works for the good of those who love him, who have been called according to his purpose" (Romans 8:28, italics mine). If you have to leave the mission field because of circumstances beyond your control, embrace the truth of this verse. God is at work, regardless of your circumstance, and He will be faithful to you. You must recognize that fact in your life lest you be overcome with disappointment and bitterness about leaving. If left unchecked, that disappointment and bitterness will mock your every attempt to adjust to life back home

The Guilt of Going Home

It is obvious to anyone who has spent time on the mission field that the laborers are few. Missionaries usually work long, hard hours, yet there always seems so much more that needs to be done. In thinking of leaving the mission field, it is easy to feel a sense of guilt about going, especially when going home means leaving work undone, or increasing the workload your co-workers must carry.

If left unchecked, false guilt or condemnation over leaving the mission field can become a paralyzing, depressing force, especially in the period just before your departure and immediately after your arrival home.

It is helpful to remember, however, that missionaries seldom have the opportunity to leave with their work completed. Most of a missionary's job involves working with people, and people are in a constant state of change. Instead of focusing on having to leave work unfinished, focus on whether it is God's will for you to leave. If it is God's will for you to leave, you must put your trust in Him. God will take care of what you cannot. He is bigger than your ministry responsibilities, and He can and will raise up other workers to take your place. He wants your trust to be in Him.

Jeff's experience illustrates this point well. Jeff was the head of food services at a large Christian camping and convention center. It was a demanding job, but Jeff handled it with ease and enjoyment. The camp had an effective ministry, with many teenagers coming to know Christ as a result of the summer camping program.

It came as a total surprise to Jeff when he felt God directing him to a new ministry in a different direction. He struggled for days with it. He knew the scarcity of trained and experienced food service people, and he knew his departure would create a hole that would be difficult to fill. As a result, he began feeling a sense of guilt about leaving. He put off handing in his resignation, but finally felt he had to do it. While the director encouraged Jeff in his obedience to the will of God, there was no hiding his disappointment over the resignation. Of course, this heightened the sense of guilt Jeff already felt.

The very next day, the director burst into the kitchen. "Look at this," he excitedly called to Jeff. "It's a letter from a man who served as a chef in the military. He wants to know if we have any positions available in food services. Look at his qualifications! In all my years in Christian camping, I have never had anyone with such great qualifications write and ask for a job."

As Jeff scanned the letter, he felt embarrassed. He had focused so much of his energy in fretting over and feeling guilty about leaving that he had neglected to put his trust in God, whom he knew was calling him in a new direction.

The week before Jeff finally left his job, his replacement started work. Jeff was able to give him some orientation, and it was a quick and easy transition.

There is absolutely no need to experience guilt about leaving the mission field in the will of God. Your confidence is in God, and He will provide. There are many legitimate things to be concerned about in preparing for a return home, but guilt is not one of them.

Ideals and Relationships

Most missionaries arrive on the mission field with a high level of idealism. Ideals are wonderful, but they are just that: ideals. All too often, our ideals form the basis of our expectations. We expect our fellow missionaries will have a certain level of maturity or will behave in a certain way. We expect the mission agency to function in a particular manner. We also expect God to do many wonderful things through our ministry as we step out in faith to serve Him. Usually our expectations are overinflated, and need to be modified to be realistic. For some who have arrived on the mission field full of idealism, this can be a shattering experience which can lead to bitterness and resentment toward the mission agency and toward

fellow missionaries who fail to meet their expectations.

It is not necessarily wrong to be disappointed
when expectations are not met. But it is wrong to
let that disappointment fester into bitterness and
resentment toward your fellow workers. Missionaries are human, and mission agencies are imperfect institutions. Working on the mission field
is a high-pressure lifestyle. People are working in
difficult situations, and are often cut off from their
culture, family, and friends.

In such an environment, it is to be expected
that mistakes and misunderstandings will occur.
The key is to resolve these when they occur, and
not let them develop into major interpersonal conflicts. Tragically, that is what often happens. As a
result, conflict with fellow workers continues to be
the major reason why most missionaries leave the
mission field prematurely. You must be sure it is
not your motivation for leaving.

As you contemplate leaving the mission field,
are you harboring bitterness in your heart toward
your mission agency or fellow workers? If so, are
you prepared to deal with it? Perhaps you need to
seek forgiveness from a fellow worker or mission
director for *your* attitude toward them. If there is
still open and unresolved conflict between you and
someone in the mission, try to find a neutral
person who can help resolve the conflict by talking
things out with those involved. The Bible is explicit
about the need to maintain good interpersonal
relationships between fellow Christians.

Perhaps you are afraid to attempt reconciliation, because you don't think the other party will
be interested. Go ahead anyway, and you may be
pleasantly surprised by the other person's open-

ness. Even if your fears prove to be true, you have tried to follow the instruction of the writer to the Hebrews who said, "Make every effort to live in peace with all men..." (Hebrews 12:14). If you must leave behind a rift in any relationship, make sure it is one that you have done your best to mend.

If you leave the mission field with bitterness and unresolved conflict, it will be a stumbling block to you for the rest of your life, or until you finally face it and deal with it. It will be like a hook buried deep in your heart which Satan will continually jerk to bring you under condemnation. So don't, under any circumstance, leave the mission field with bitterness and unresolved conflict.

Once More around the Mountain

Have you heard the saying, "once more around the mountain"? The saying comes from the experience of the Israelites after they escaped from Egypt. God had to extend their sojourn in the wilderness again and again, because they were not ready to enter the Promised Land. They seemed unable to learn the lesson of obedience to God. What about you? Have you learned the lessons God wanted you to learn while on the mission field? If you haven't, He will continually bring similar situations into your life until you finally learn the lesson. Some people expend a tremendous amount of energy trudging around the mountain instead of moving up it!

As you come to the close of your time on the mission field, be sure that God won't have to send you around the mountain again. Graciously learn the lessons He has prepared for your spiritual growth. Ask Him to reveal to you any hidden areas in your life that need to be dealt with. In bringing

closure to your time on the mission field, your aim
must be to leave with a clean heart before the Lord,
a clean slate with your co-workers, and with their
blessing, if possible.

Also remember that some may have gone to the
mission field to escape a bad situation or an unresolved conflict. Unfortunately, physical distance
is not emotional distance, and the circumstances
you left behind probably have not been far from
your mind during your time away. Rest assured
that God will have those same situations waiting
for you when you get home. He is a God who wants
His children to face their failures, and to deal with
them with His help. He will not allow His children
to hide from their weaknesses and failures, but
will continue to bring us face to face with our
weaknesses and failures until we deal with them.
In the process, we will learn much about Him and
about ourselves.

If you are on the mission field, and are aware
of any broken relationships, unresolved conflicts,
and other such situations, begin to deal with them
before you leave for home. Don't procrastinate or
promise yourself that you will make everything
right the moment you step off the airplane. You
may not have the opportunity to do so. Act now.
Write to the person concerned in the situation, or
call and talk to them about it. How you do it is not
as important as making an effort at reconciliation.

A good place to start in this process is prayer.
Take time to lay your situation honestly before
God. He will not condemn you if there are things
that must be dealt with. Rather, He will work with
you, and will reveal to you ways to handle these
situations once and for all. If you find you are
unable to face something on your own, seek out a

friend you can confide in and pray with, or someone who can give you helpful advice and counsel.

Get Debriefed!

No, this has nothing to do with removing a portion of your clothing! It's a process of sitting down with your leader and going over a number of points that will allow you to reflect on your time on the mission field. You can make some assessments of your effectiveness during that time, and can identify both the things you think you did right and the things you think you did wrong, or which were not effective. It is also a time for sharing any insights you may have gained that will help fellow workers in the years to come. Debriefing is a vital, but sadly neglected, part of the closure process.

Because debriefing is so often overlooked, I have included a debriefing outline as an appendix. If your leader is unfamiliar with the process, you can show him this outline. In most cases, leaders will be happy to provide you with the opportunity for a debriefing once they understand the process.

If the opportunity is not available, it is possible to conduct your own debriefing. You will need a Bible, a notebook, and any diaries you may have kept. The personal debriefing goes like this:

Set aside a time for reflection on Philippians 4:8-9: "Finally, brothers, whatever is true, whatever is noble, whatever is right, whatever is pure, whatever is lovely, whatever is admirable—if anything is excellent or praiseworthy—think about such things. Whatever you have learned or received or heard from me, or seen in me—put it into practice. And the God of peace will be with you." Using this verse as a springboard, spend two or three hours alone, reflecting on your missions experience.

As you reflect, make a list of the things you are grateful to God for during your time on the mission field. List them under the headings of true, noble, right, pure, lovely, and admirable.

In your notebook, record the following:

- What you have learned through your experience on the mission field.

- What you have received from God through it.

- What you have seen in the lives of your fellow workers that you would like to incorporate into your life.

- What you have seen God do in the lives of the people to whom you ministered.

Pray and ask God to show you how you can work these new insights and values into your life once you are back home. Record the specific insights He shows you.

List the obstacles that might prevent you from incorporating these new values and insights into your life. Pray about strategies to overcome them.

Finally, write yourself a letter. Pretend you are writing the letter to a friend, and include in it the most important points you have covered in your personal debriefing. Put the letter in an envelope, and address it to your permanent home address. Ask a reliable friend to mail the letter to you in five or six months' time. When it arrives, it will be a surprise, and should be a great encouragement to you. You will also be able to measure just how well you are doing in applying to your life at home all the things you learned on the mission field. Covenant with yourself that when you receive the letter, you will correct any deviation that may have crept in from the course you set for your life.

It is important to leave the mission field with a clean heart and a clear slate. If you want to experience a good and positive transition from the mission field to home, you have no alternative but to work these issues through. It may require great humility on your part to resolve some situations, but the rewards of doing so are well worth it.

This is not all that is involved in the closure process; it is merely the part that requires you to look inward and assess the state of your heart before the Lord and your fellow workers. After the reflection involved in the debriefing process, begin assessing just how much you have changed while you have been away, as well as how much your home setting has changed.

2

Checklist

Young men marching off to war to fight a common enemy have always brought patriotism to the fore. So it was when multiplied thousands of young American men left for Vietnam to fight the menacing forces of communism. While their farewell was filled with patriotism, excitement, and good will, their return was anything but.

They came back to a deeply divided nation. Some quarters of the nation booed, jeered, and reviled them as traitors; other quarters praised them as heroes with brass bands and parades. With the veterans feeling alienated and alone, it took years before many of them came to terms with their experience. Some never have.

Why did these soldiers go through this experience upon their return home? The answer is not simple; many complex historical and political forces played into the situation. But I believe one of the reasons these soldiers suffered what they did upon their return home was that they had not properly prepared for what awaited them. They had not adequately considered how much *they* had changed in their time away, and how much the society at home had changed.

Most of them left as raw recruits, eighteen or nineteen years old, straight out of school. They returned at the end of their tour of duty as hardened, battle-weary men. They had seen and done things in Vietnam that had changed their lives forever. Indeed, in life experience, they returned old beyond their years.

In the turbulent and changing 1960s and early 1970s, two years was a long time to be away. Much had changed in two years. The cause for which they had gone to fight had fallen into disfavor at home. Young people calling for an end to the war clashed head-on with police and National Guardsmen in the streets. A number of people lost their lives in the course of opposing the war. Deep divisions had occurred in American society. Into this vortex, the unwary Vietnam veterans returned, expecting a hero's welcome. Their hopes were most often dashed.

Had these soldiers taken time before leaving Vietnam to assess both the changes that had taken place in them and the changes that had occurred at home, they would have been better prepared to handle what was coming. They could have anticipated how people might react to them, and could have taken the necessary steps to soften the emotional blow of such reactions.

As a returning missionary, you must learn from this experience. Things have not been stagnant during your time away. It is imperative before you leave the mission field to take time to properly assess how much you have changed, and how much things have changed back home.

Never presume that no changes have occurred, even if you have only been away on a one-month outreach. Nothing stays the same, neither you nor the people you left at home. Humans exist in a state of constant change in which they are seeing and learning new things and adjusting to them.

If you could put the process of change on hold while you are away, the re-entry process would be simple. But you cannot, and because of the changes that take place during your absence, the re-entry process becomes a potential mine field through which you must navigate.

Set aside some time before you leave the mission field to try to assess what changes have occurred in your life during your absence from home. You may find it helpful to look back over your prayer journal or diary. Read over the entries you have made during your time on the mission field. Then read some of the earlier entries you made before you left home.

Are you the same person you were back then? How have you changed? Are there any specific experiences that have caused your life to change? What are those experiences? Was their impact on your life positive or negative? How do you think people back home are going to react to these changes in you? Ask such questions of yourself, noting in your journal any insights you come up with in the process.

I have listed some changes that could have occurred, and have tried to anticipate possible reactions to these changes. This checklist is by no means comprehensive, and is provided only by way of example to get you thinking.

Physical

You may have experienced no significant physical change during your time away. Most missionaries, though, go through some changes. You may have had to alter your hair style and appearance in keeping with the culture in which you have been working. Often the rigors of the mission field mean that missionaries are a lot fitter and trimmer when they come home. On the other hand, some may have struggled with sickness and disease, and may appear frail and gaunt. If you have been on the mission field for a number of years since your last visit home, then, of course, you will have aged. A few wrinkles may even have appeared! Perhaps the jet-black hair you left home with has turned gray, or your flowing locks may have become wispy tufts gallantly clinging to the crown of your head.

Whatever the change, people are going to notice. If you have begun to go bald or have added wrinkles while away, come to terms with it. People are going to notice and comment on the fact—often in unflattering ways.

Jan had been a missionary in northern India for two years, and had survived mainly on a diet of rice and soup. As a result, Jan, who had always struggled with being overweight, arrived home slim and trim. The anticipated comments were forthcoming. People remarked on how good she looked. Jan bought new clothes, since her old ones were now too big. As a result, she felt good about herself and her appearance. Then she encountered a response that she hadn't anticipated. Mamma! Reaching back into her Italian heritage, Mamma had decided Jan looked sickly, and needed to be fattened up! She began preparing big meals for Jan, and encouraged her to eat up. Jan resisted at first, but because her weight loss had occurred as a result of heat, sickness, and meager food rations in India, and not because of a real change in eating habits, she soon found herself returning to her old ways of eating. Desserts, which she had done without for two years, were now a regular part of a meal. Soon Jan had gained forty pounds and returned to the weight she was before leaving for India. None of her new clothes fitted her, and she became very depressed.

How have *you* changed physically? Are they permanent changes, or, like Jan, are they likely to reverse themselves after time at home? Of course, some missionaries arrive home in desperate need of fattening up. Whatever the change, try as accurately as possible to anticipate the reaction of various people to it. That way you will be able to prepare yourself for their comments and reactions, and in some cases, head them off.

Social

Sometimes social and emotional changes are the hardest to gauge. They are often more subtle and less obvious than physical changes. It may be that you will not fully realize the extent of the change until you get home. As you measure yourself socially and emotionally against your peers, you get a better idea of the changes that have taken place in your life.

One change you will probably notice is a much greater understanding and acceptance of people from other races and ethnic groups. You have become less "ethnocentric." This means that the dogmas and practices of your culture are not as central or absolute to you as they used to be; now you can easily embrace other cultural perspectives and ways of doing things.

It is easy to anticipate that there may be some conflict with friends and family back home over this change, especially if you come from an area where people are ethnocentric and biased, perhaps even discriminatory, against other races. It is possible that you could be ridiculed for your willingness to embrace other races and their cultural perspectives.

Emotional

One of the biggest changes you may experience is a change in emotional attachments in your relationships. You may find that when you arrive home, you are no longer as closely bonded to certain people. Part of being human is developing emotional attachments to others. As a child, you bonded to your parents, then close friends, and perhaps finally to a marriage partner. Time away can alter the way you think and feel about many of those relationships. You change and form new emotional attachments to people in your new setting. But so do those you left behind. So when you return home, you may find you are no longer close to your best friend, boyfriend, or girlfriend. This doesn't mean that you are no longer friends, just that the level of emotional attachment in the relationship has diminished. Likewise, you may discover that new relationships develop with people to whom you were not previously close.

All this is quite natural. People who leave home to attend college, take an out-of-town job, or join the military will experience the same thing upon their return home. The important point to note in returning home is that people often are not prepared for these changes. As a result, misunderstandings and hurts can occur. People may think you are snubbing or ignoring them. It may take some time for them to realize that both of you have changed, so be patient.

Political

It is quite possible that you have changed politically while you have been away. It will not necessarily be a shift in your political party allegiance, but more a change in the way you view issues.

Ron was an Australian working among the poor in an overcrowded slum area of Manila. He was no friend of communism, but as he spent time among these people and saw the hopelessness and desperation they lived with each day, Ron began to understand the power and appeal of the Communist insurgency taking place in the Philippines at the time. He understood how and why these people grasped with all their might onto the Communists' rhetoric and empty promises. It was the only hope these people saw! Ron was in no way persuaded to endorse what these insurgents were doing; he simply understood them and their popularity a little better.

Also in the Philippines was Anna, an American missionary ministering among the prostitutes of Olongapo City. Until 1992, the United States Naval Base at Subic Bay was located outside Olongapo City, and American sailors were the most frequent customers of the very prostitutes Anna was trying to reach with the Gospel. Anna was sickened to her stomach one night as she encountered a U.S. sailor in full dress uniform walking out of a bar. He was dragging a leash behind him, and attached to the other end of it were two teenage prostitutes, chained to each other at the wrists.

Appalled with the behavior of the sailors who represented her country's government, Anna was forced to face the image of "the ugly American."

She was ashamed of her country for the first time.

Nothing can produce a more volatile argument than a political discussion. If you have experienced things that have changed some of your political understandings or views, keep them to yourself. Don't go home and announce that your country's form of government or foreign policy is wrong, especially if you know it will stir controversy. If the right opportunity arises for you to share some of your political observations, do so humbly and without contention. Your aim should be to help others understand why you have arrived at your conclusions, not to try to show others how much superior and enlightened your views are compared to theirs.

Spiritual

There is going to be the obvious spiritual growth and development that occurs in the course of time spent on the mission field. However, many missionaries, especially those serving with interdenominational missions, are exposed to a wide range of theological perspectives. We all have our particular theological views which are often derived from our denominational background and understanding of the Bible. Theological perspectives are good and necessary. But there are as many of them as there are denominations. In the course of your work on the mission field, you may have served with others who have very different theological views from your own. Such interaction usually serves to broaden you. You may have become more responsive to and accepting of other doctrinal points of view.

Like political convictions, people tend to hold tightly to their theological convictions. While it is healthy to broaden your theological viewpoint while on the mission field, it is not your place to impose your new insights upon others when you return home. If you go home seeking to change the convictions of people in your church, you are likely to meet with a negative, even hostile response. So be wise in how you share things that to some people will only signify the dilution of your faith, or worse yet, the error of your faith.

Financial

The reality of any financial decisions you made prior to leaving for the mission field will affect you upon your return home. If you sold a home before leaving, the reality of that decision may have not yet affected you, since adequate housing may always have been provided by the mission agency during your tenure of service. But the reality of the decision will hit as you "camp out" with your family or in a friend's home and ponder your long-term housing needs.

I recently met a young woman missionary from the Pacific Islands. She told me that because she had been away from home for so long that she had forfeited her right to own land on her island. Knowing that she would never be a landowner herself, it was very difficult for her to visit her brothers and sisters and see them building and developing their land. She had to deal with feelings of jealousy and resentment.

Likewise, you may find it difficult to see people at home who have prospered financially while you seem to have gone backward as a result of going to the mission field. You may well have to overcome your own resentment and jealousy.

When my wife Donna returned to Canada and

visited her sisters in their beautiful homes, she had to make a deliberate decision to remember that God is just in all His ways, and that the most important thing is to live in obedience to Him. For us, that meant the "gypsy" lifestyle we had been living; for her sisters, it meant being settled and prospering. They weren't wrong in having beautiful homes, and we weren't crazy for selling ours and giving the proceeds to missions.

People at home who do not understand your motivation for going to the mission field may well think, and tell you, that you are a "sucker" for giving up so much, especially in the area of financial security. And don't be surprised if some of these people are from your church! Friends and family may even resent having to help you financially. So be prepared for some testing in this area.

Changes at Home

Having assessed some of the changes that have taken place in you, it is time to turn your attention toward home. What has happened in your home country during the time you've been away? What has happened in your home town? Your church? Your family? Take time to think about the changes that have occurred, and their implications upon your return.

Remember Sergei Krikalev, the Soviet cosmonaut we mentioned in the introduction? During his ten months in space, his nation ceased to exist. He lifted off as a Soviet citizen, and came down as a citizen of Russia. And not only that, but his home town—Leningrad—had changed its name to St. Petersburg. That's some change to adjust to!

Elaine was a missionary from New Zealand. After serving on the mission field for five years, she returned home for a six-month furlough. During the five years Elaine had been away, there had been a change of government in her country. "Governments change all the time, so I didn't really think much about it," she confided. "But when I got home, I couldn't believe the change. The economy was bad, and people were gloomy. It seemed to take all my effort to get people to talk about anything other than how bad things were. It's like they were down in the basements of their lives digging holes. It was very depressing, and took some getting used to."

Don't be caught unaware. Take some time to contemplate how the changes that have occurred at home in your absence may affect you and your re-entry.

Family Changes

Depending on how long you have been away, there may have been major changes in your family. Some of the changes, like the marriage of a brother or sister or the birth of nieces or nephews, may be cause for belated rejoicing and celebrating. Changes like a death in the family may be more difficult for you.

When we were in Asia, we received word that Donna's father had passed away. Because of the distance and our circumstances, it was impossible for Donna to get home in time for the funeral. When she did arrive, most of the family and friends had dispersed, so she had to work through the stages of grief largely on her own. A videotape of the service was of great help in the process.

If a significant person in your life has passed away while you have been on the mission field, be prepared for a flood of emotions to hit you when

you arrive home, even if a considerable amount of
time has elapsed since their death.

Other Changes

While on the topic of change, it is time to take
stock of other differences that will occur as you
step from the mission field back into your home
culture. The life you leave behind on the mission
field is very different from what you will encounter
upon your return home. You will be moving:

- From being primarily concerned with the
  spiritual to being primarily concerned
  with practical matters.

- From being daily surrounded with
  Christian encouragement and fellowship
  to deriving your fellowship and
  encouragement from Wednesday evening
  and Sunday morning church services.

- From having a fixed and measurable goal
  to perhaps having none at all.

- From seeing abject poverty firsthand to
  perhaps experiencing seemingly
  overwhelming wealth.

- From a high degree of self-motivation to
  searching for new motivation.

- From being somebody special in the
  culture in which you were serving to being
  nobody special.

- From serving with people who have a
  world perspective to being with people
  who, in many cases, do not care much for
  those outside their own circle.

This list is by no means exhaustive. But all of these are very real issues of change with which you will have to grapple as you re-enter your home culture. Start to think about these changes and their implications in your situation. Pray and ask God to reveal to you some strategies that will help lessen their impact upon you.

Re-Entry Stress

With the knowledge of the changes that have occurred in you, the changes that have occurred at home, and some of the changes you will experience after your return home, you are in a better place to understand the elements that interplay to create re-entry stress.

Re-entry stress can take the form of feeling disorientated and out of place; feeling disillusioned; feeling irritated with others and with certain aspects of your culture; or feeling lonely, isolated, depressed, and misunderstood.

The extent to which you are affected by these symptoms is dependent upon a number of factors. Some of these factors are the nature of your relationship with the host culture you have been working in; your relationship to your own culture; personal characteristics; and the amount of change that has occurred in your life and at home. Listed below are fifteen questions to help you gauge whether you are in for a rough landing or a relatively smooth one upon your re-entry.[1]

Work through the points. Read them. Think about them, then write down your answers and observations in your notebook or journal. You may also want to have each member of your family work through the points.

A Personal Assessment

Host Country

1. How long have you been away from your home country?

2. In what ways have you identified with the host culture?

3. In what ways are the host culture and your culture similar and dissimilar (e.g., climate, geography, language, religion, standard of living, ethnic groups, politics, dress, customs)?

4. How fulfilled do you feel in your overseas work and experience? What has it been like for you?

5. What will it be like to be away from the host culture (i.e., friends, places, ministry)?

Personal Characteristics

6. Describe your physical health (e.g., stamina, nutrition, eating habits, stress levels, exercise).

7. Identify and jot down some personal qualities that may help or hinder your adjustment.

8. Have you noticed any important changes in who you are since living abroad? List them.

9. Describe any important transitions you or a family member are going through (e.g., marriage, children leaving home, entering mid-life or retirement, births, deaths, or even divorce).

10. In what ways are you preparing for your return home?

Home Culture

11. How long will you be staying home?

12. Describe the primary purposes or expectations for your return.

13. What have any previous re-entry experiences been like?

14. To what extent have you stayed updated on events and changes back home (i.e., reading, news, letters, phone calls)?

15. Describe the quality of your support groups in your home country (family, friends, church).

Of course, there are no right or wrong answers to any of these. They are provided simply to help you focus on a number of factors that are important to the re-entry process. Through serious consideration of these points, you will get some idea of the re-entry stress that may lie ahead of you. To be forewarned is to be forearmed! To be aware of the challenges you face upon your return home is to avoid being totally overcome by them when they occur. If you see that you are going to experience a high degree of re-entry stress, do not become disheartened. Be assured that God is greater than your greatest challenge. Meditate on God's promise to you, which He first spoke to the Children of Israel prior to their entrance into the Promised Land: "I will not, I will not, I will not in any degree leave you helpless, nor forsake nor let you down, relax My hold on you.—Assuredly not!" (Hebrews 13:5, Amp.).

3

Winding Down

As the astronaut's craft begins its descent, it is time to take care of practical matters. It is time to make sure everything on board is properly stowed for re-entry, and to ensure that all systems are functioning properly. It is also time to make sure that all emergency equipment is ready, and that the astronaut himself is securely strapped into his seat. Re-entering the earth's atmosphere can be perilous and turbulent.

So it is for you as your time on the mission field draws to a close. It is time to decay your trajectory and begin inching out of the orbit of missions. In the process of doing so, there are a number of practical matters that need your attention.

Start Delegating Your Work

Many people find that as their attention is drawn toward returning home, they begin to feel distanced from the mission field. Their thoughts begin to revolve more and more around going home—what it will be like and what they will do once they get there—and less and less around their work on the mission field. This is natural. It is part of the process God uses to wean people from their present circumstances and prepare them for the next step He has for their lives. So if you are planning to return home, and you find yourself becoming less emotionally involved in your mission work, relax! Begin to slow down and let others start taking over your responsibilities.

This doesn't mean that you slow down in the area of your personal relationship with God. Quite the contrary. Given the re-entry stress you are going to experience upon your return home, your relationship with the Lord needs to be stronger than ever. It simply means you begin to "wind down" in relation to your work responsibilities.

If another missionary is coming to take over your ministry, do everything possible to see that he or she is properly trained and prepared for the task ahead. If you will be leaving before your replacement arrives, make sure you leave things in order, recording in a notebook anything that you think will be of value to him in carrying on where you left off. Proverbs 22:1 says, "A good name is more desirable than great riches; to be esteemed is better than silver or gold." In moving out of your mission field responsibilities, plan to do all you can to leave a good name behind you.

If you are on a short-term missions outreach, each member of the team will face the tendency to wind down individually and corporately. Care must be taken to ensure that everyone doesn't wind down so much that nothing gets done!

Attend to Medical Needs

If you have any ongoing illnesses, seek medical attention before leaving for home (unless you are returning home for health reasons). Secure a copy of your medical records, including a list of any medications you were prescribed, and any unusual illnesses or diseases to which you have been exposed. It is also a good idea to keep a record of any medical concerns you may have, so you can consult with a physician regarding them upon your return home.

While on the mission field, your body may have become the focus of attention for a large number of interesting critters. Some may have even taken up residence on or in your body! Arriving home with leeches hanging on your legs, lice swarming in your hair, and parasites and worms residing in the warm crevices of your digestive tract is to guarantee yourself a negative re-entry experience!

Not everyone is going to welcome you into their home with open arms in such a condition. So if it is appropriate to your situation, go to a pharmacy before you leave, and get some de-worming medicine and de-lousing shampoo and use them. While parasites, lice, and worms are a fact of life in many parts of the mission field, they are best left there.

Return Bearing Gifts

As your time to leave for home approaches, give some thought to the kinds of gifts you are going to take home. The best are those which are native to the country or region in which you have been serving, and which have been made by local craftsmen. Such gifts are unique, and relay some small part of the culture of your host nation. They also are a good interest point through which you can share more about the culture.

However, a word of caution here. Many missionaries have brought home "quaint" souvenirs without realizing the spiritual significance placed upon them by the local religion and culture. Be careful not to bring these items with you.

In addition to obtaining gifts for your family, friends, and supporters, make sure you bring something for your pastor and/or youth leader. It is also a good idea to stock up on a quantity of inexpensive, small gifts. Then if you are asked to share in a Sunday school class, you will be able to leave a small reminder of your visit with them. Pencils, bookmarks, local candies, calendars, and postcards are excellent items for such times.

You Are a Tangible Link

After your arrival home, *you* become a tangible link between the people and culture you have been working in and the Christians in your home church and other churches in your area. You can be a strategic bridge through which God can bring greater awareness, understanding and insight of another culture, as well as motivating other Christians to go to the mission field. With this responsibility in mind, begin thinking about ways you can accomplish this.

The things that have become so familiar to you during your time on the mission field will seem very strange to the people back home. Simple things, such as how the language sounds, will be of interest to them. Before returning home, take a tape recorder to church and record some worship songs and hymns in the native language. You could also record someone reading from the Bible and saying a few simple phrases in their language.

You may like to plan a small display board with photos of the local people and places on it. (If this is not your "thing," ask someone who is creative to help you. It will be well worth it.) Have some of the people write a little about themselves underneath their photos. Ask them to write in their native language and provide an English translation below. Remember, the aim is not to present a visually perfect display, but a record of real people and how their lives have been affected by the Gospel. You may also like to add a copy of your daily schedule and a brief outline of your ministry or job responsibilities while on the mission field. A simple display such as this can be an effective tool for God to use to speak to others about the challenge of missions.

You might plan a small slide show that takes your audience through a typical day on the mission field. Take your camera with you, and record your day on film. You may prefer to use a video camera, giving a commentary as you go along, and conducting short interviews with fellow workers and those to whom you are ministering. But remember to keep it interesting and to the point.

Something else you may wish to consider is taking part or all of a national costume home with you. You can hang the costume beside your display board at the back of the church; being dressed in the national costume while giving your presentations can have great visual effect. Of course, this approach is not recommended if the national dress is a banana leaf loincloth!

On one occasion, Donna and I were given "fine mats"—beautiful handwoven mats painstakingly created by Pacific Island women—which had value beyond money. They were presented to us to take back to our home church in Montreal, Canada as a gift of appreciation for them allowing us to go out as missionaries.

There are so many creative ways to bring a little of the mission field home. Perhaps some of the people you have been working among would like a pen pal from your home church. You could have your church adopt a Sunday school class on the mission field, providing them with materials and supplies. The opportunities are unlimited!

Before you leave, make a list of items needed by your fellow missionaries. If part of the work of your mission involves a medical clinic, ask the nurse or doctor who staffs the clinic for a list of the things they routinely run out of. (Be prepared for a long list!) When you get home, you may be able to arrange for an individual, church, or business to donate some of these items to the clinic.

If your mission has any literature (brochures, newsletters, articles, calendars) relating to the area in which you have been serving, bring some home with you. Such information is helpful in exposing other Christians to the challenge of missions while giving more insight into where you have been and what you have been doing.

One couple (who attended a YWAM mission training school and then spent several months on a short-term outreach) purchased video recordings of the teaching delivered in their training school, and donated them to their church library. This had a double blessing; it provided some good teaching on missions for members of the church while helping them understand what this couple had experienced in their time away.

If videos are not practical for you, books about missions, or those written by leaders within your mission, serve a similar purpose. You may also wish to bring with you some general information books about the country or area in which you were serving. These books can be donated to the church library for the benefit of all the congregation.

Start a Journal

You may not think keeping a journal is your thing, but I would encourage you to try and do so, especially during your transition time. The value of keeping a journal during this time is both spiritual and practical.

It is likely that as you plan your return home, God will reveal to you many insights to guide you along the way. These insights can be recorded in your journal, and will become a solace to you when you feel no one understands you or the things you've been through. It will be your companion through the time of re-entry adjustment. When your faith is wavering, it will be a constant reminder to you that God promises to "give you hope and a future" (Jeremiah 29:11).

Your journal is also a good place to record practical information about life on the mission field which you want to remember after your return home. You might want to include notes on such things as a typical day for you on the mission field, notes on your debriefing time, or a summary of your ministry.

All of this will serve as good resource material for you later as you work through re-entry and share your experiences with others.

Prepare People for Your Return

The apostle Paul made many missionary forays into new territory. After each journey, he returned to his home church to encourage the Christians, and to recruit some of them to accompany him on his next adventure. Here is an account of one of those returns: "On arriving there [Antioch], they gathered the church together and reported all that

God had done through them and how he had
opened the door of faith to the Gentiles. And they
stayed there a long time with the disciples" (Acts
14:27-28).

Recorded here is the ideal situation for a returning missionary, in which he is given the opportunity to share with the entire church about
his mission experience. But unless your ministry
has a high profile like Paul's, it is unlikely that the
entire church will gather to hear your stories of life
on the mission field and watch your out-of-focus
slides! In fact, many of the returning missionaries
to whom I have spoken were shocked at the lack
of interest their home church showed in them, and
have become bitterly disillusioned. You do not
want this to happen to you, so take the initiative
to ensure that it doesn't.

A good point to keep in mind regarding expectations about your return home is that the degree
to which your church welcomes you back is in a
large part dependent upon how you left. If you
tended to circulate at the periphery of your church
and then drifted into missions, it is unlikely the
church will be very informed about or interested
in your return. Likewise, if you have failed to keep
your church informed about you and your ministry during your time away, they will have little idea
of what you have been through, and therefore have
little empathy with you upon your return. A
church can be like a family. If you left your church
estranged, you will most likely return to the same
estranged relationship.

All these situations tend to be more indicative
of the short-term mission setting, where it is easy
to slip out of church and off to the mission field
for six months or a year. Longer term missionaries

usually need to be recommended and supported by their home church, so they tend to leave in good relationship with their church. Still, a long-term missionary's failure to communicate adequately with his home church during his time on the mission field will make it harder to arouse their interest upon his return.

You can greatly enhance the reception you receive from your home church by planning for your homecoming. This may sound premeditated or even presumptuous, but if you do not plan and share your expectations with people at home, most likely things will not work out the way you want them to. Notice that when Paul and Barnabas returned to Antioch, *they* called the people together. Paul orchestrated the whole thing. I am not saying to go over your pastor's head, but don't sit back and expect to have all your dreams about returning to your home church fulfilled. You must take the initiative! Make sure your church is informed about when you are coming home, the type of opportunities for sharing you would welcome, and the person who is coordinating your schedule.

One enterprising young lady wanted the opportunity to speak in front of her whole church, but realized that the pastor was not comfortable with handing the pulpit over to a lay person. So she wrote and told him what she had been doing. She included a list of questions he might like to ask her in an interview, with a brief idea of the kind of answers she would give to the questions. This worked out wonderfully. The pastor agreed to interview her one Sunday morning, and while he maintained "control" of the situation, she was able to share about what she had seen and done.

I was impressed with her attitude. She didn't

give up and say, "My pastor never lets anyone speak on Sunday morning." Instead, she found a solution to the problem. There are ways around difficulties, if you pray hard and look for them!

If you will be arriving home sick or burned-out, let your church and your family know so they can properly plan for your return. People are not mind-readers. If you don't share your expectations, they are not likely to be met, and you may feel bitter and disappointed at God, your friends, and your family. If you share your expectations with others, they will soon tell you if they are realistic or not. Many returning missionaries suffer needlessly during the re-entry period, because they have not planned ahead. They have not shared their expectations with others. How can you avoid this? Start now by sharing with friends and family what you would like to occur upon your arrival home.

––––––––––

To put this process of closure in perspective, let me say that closure is like passing on the baton in a relay race.

On television, I watched the final of the men's 4-by-100-meter relay at the 1992 Summer Olympics in Barcelona. Top athletes from around the world hunkered down in their starting blocks, waiting for the race to begin. They finally were called to their marks. They hunched forward, their legs set, ready for the sound of the starter's pistol. The crack of the gun reverberated throughout the stadium as each runner lunged forward, gathering speed with every step.

Within seconds, the leading runners were pounding down the straight toward the finish line. In just a few fleeting moments it was over. Each runner dashed one hundred meters. Three times the baton had been faultlessly passed. When it was all over, the American team had done it better and faster than anyone had done it before. They had made it look so simple. They were the Olympic and World champions, and took their places atop the podium to receive their gold medals.

The mission field is like that race. <u>God calls us to run a leg of the race</u>. In running our leg, we join the ranks of a long and illustrious line of people God has called to carry the baton in reaching the lost of the world with the Gospel. There are those for whom running a leg of the relay has meant a lifetime of faithful service on the mission field. For others, it has been several years, while some were called only for the short-term. The length of time for which God has called you to serve is not important. What *is* important is that you serve diligently to the best of your abilities. When that period comes to a close, it is time to pass the baton on to the next person God has called.

That is closure. It is ending your leg of the relay and handing your ministry responsibilities to those who follow. In many cases, this is another person. In some cases, no one will come to follow on where you have left off. In that case, you must pass the baton on to the Holy Spirit to continue the work that was begun in the hearts of the people to whom you ministered. Closure is simply closing out your leg of the race. It is bringing your time on the mission field to an end emotionally, spiritually, socially, and physically.

This does not necessarily mean that you will never again be involved in missions. It simply means that you have brought to a proper close that passage of time on the mission field that has gone before. You have released it, and it has released you. You are free to move into the next passage of life God has for you.

Once you have brought to conclusion your time on the mission field you are ready for re-entry. Just like the space shuttle re-entering the earth's atmosphere, you are in for an exciting ride. There is likely to be some turbulence and heat along the way. But that is natural. That is part of the process. Do not be alarmed. With God's help, you can navigate your way through it. Navigating the re-entry process is the focus of the rest of this book.

Part Two:

Re-Entry

4

Final Approach

The airplane finally lifts off; you're on your way home. As it climbs to 33,000 feet and heads out over the Pacific Ocean, you think back over your year of missionary service in Indonesia. It was a challenging, exciting, life-changing time. As a result of your ministry, you saw a number of people accept Jesus Christ as their Lord. You made many new friends among both the Indonesians and those with whom you were serving. There were many tearful goodbyes.

You're now four hours out over the Pacific, and your mind switches from reviewing how things had been in Indonesia to contemplating how things will be when you get home. Your excitement rises as you imagine seeing family and friends again. Your mind conjures up many images. You think how great it will be to sit down to dinner with some of your close friends and share your experiences with them, challenging them to go to the mission field, too. You can almost see the crowd waiting to welcome you at the airport. You see yourself standing before the church on Sunday morning giving a full report on your ministry.

As the airplane lines up for its final approach,

you're almost home, and you wonder if perhaps
there will even be a civic reception for you. Seconds later, you feel the jolt of the wheels on the
runway—you're home! As the plane taxis to a stop
at the gate, you grab your things from the over-
head locker and head for the door.

You finally make it through Immigration and
Customs and into the terminal concourse, but
there is no thronging crowd to greet you. In fact,
no one is there for you. After fighting the crowds
to collect your luggage, you wait so long that
everyone is gone, and one lone duffel bag circles
on the baggage carousel. Your parents finally show
up, apologizing and explaining how they got stuck
in traffic on the way to the airport.

There's no civic reception either, only an evening at home with your family. Your granny calls
to ask if you met any "nice girls" over there, your
mother reminds you that you'll have to find a job
soon, and your father tells you that the engine in
your car died while you were away. Your young
sister who idolized you before you left has to be
surgically separated from the television set to
spend any time with you, and your younger
brother resents having you back in "his" room.

Your heart sinks, but you hang on for church
on Sunday. At least *they* will understand all you
have been through. On Sunday morning, you slide
into the pew beside the assistant pastor. You wait
for him to ask about your ministry in Indonesia,
but he comments on your cool tan, and asks if CD
players are really as cheap over there as he heard.

As the service commences, the pastor publicly
welcomes you back. Your spirits start to climb. As
you shake the pastor's hand after church, he
doesn't ask you questions about Indonesia, but

comments on how good it is that you're back for next Saturday's work day to clean the church yard.

By Monday morning, you're totally depressed. You argue with your brother over breakfast, and your mother comments that you haven't really changed, because your room is still as messy as ever. At that point, you begin wondering why you bothered coming home at all. At least in Indonesia, people appreciated you and your ministry. The way everyone seems to be just going on with their lives here makes you feel strangely superfluous.

You feel as though you're someone who has come back from the dead; your friends and family have buried and forgotten you. You wonder if people really want you around at all, or if they would even notice if you just disappeared.

So much for your expectations. That "warm fuzzy," that chance to be pampered and to revel for a while in the afterglow of your missionary endeavor is not going to happen. Welcome to the reality of re-entry!

Where Does Your Identity Lie?

In Luke 10, we read how Jesus sent 72 people in pairs to go ahead of Him and declare His coming. Before He sent them out, He commissioned them to heal the sick and declare to people that the kingdom of God is coming.

These 72 people came back from their mission buzzing with excitement about all God had done through them. People had been healed, demons had been cast out, and they had openly and publicly declared the coming of the kingdom of God in all the villages they visited. It was heady stuff for these supposedly unlearned disciples.

When they met Jesus upon their return, everyone spoke at once, each person trying to outdo the other in sharing their fantastic exploits. "Lord, even the demons submit to us in your name," one of them shouted as he came within earshot of Jesus. Jesus waited patiently for them to quiet before He spoke. "I saw Satan fall like lightning from heaven. I have given you authority to trample on snakes and scorpions, and to overcome all the power of the enemy; nothing will harm you. However, do not rejoice that the spirits submit to you, but rejoice that your names are written in heaven" (Luke 10:17-20).

No one spoke. Wasn't He pleased with what they had done? Yes, I think He was. It was their first venture, and many wonderful things had been accomplished. Jesus wasn't negating that in any way. But He recognized that they were attempting to derive their identity from what they had done, so He moved to address that issue. He indicated that their identity came not from what they had done, but from the fact that their names were written in heaven. Or put more simply, their identity should come from who they were (children of God), and not from what they had done.

We're all like this at times. We list the things we have accomplished for God as though they were our credentials; as though our identity were dependent upon people recognizing what we have done. But the only credential that is important in the kingdom of God is that our names are written in heaven. We are sons and daughters of God. Whether we were missionaries or not has nothing to do with how God views us. He may be pleased with our diligent service, but that doesn't elevate us to the status of a privileged child. He is an impartial God and loves all His children equally

Learn to derive your identity from the fact that you are a child of God, not from the fact that you are a missionary.

Don't Be a "Special" Case

Returning missionaries often bring back an unspoken and subconscious message that they are "special," that the things they have done and learned on the mission field set them apart from other Christians who have stayed at home. Not only is such an attitude wrong, but it is also pride, and the Bible tells us that God resists the proud.

Simply because you went to the mission field does not entitle you to special treatment upon your return. It is wonderful when people recognize what you have done, and the sacrifices you have made.

But you cannot demand such treatment as your right by virtue of what you have done. You have no rights; you surrendered them to the Lord Jesus. You went to serve on the mission field out of obedience and because of your love and devotion for Him. If you went for any other reason, it was the wrong reason.

If you come home from the mission field thinking you deserve special treatment, you are going to be disappointed. The only thing the Bible declares that we deserve is judgment and separation from God. But by the grace of God, our names are written in heaven We are God's children; we do not need the approval of others for what we have done. His approval is sufficient.

Don't Be Judgmental

The apostle Paul told us, "There is one body and one Spirit—just as you were called to one hope when you were called—one Lord, one faith, one baptism; one God and Father of all, who is over all and through all and in all" (Ephesians 4:4-6). The point Paul wanted us to get is that we all have the same future and the same hope. God does not make a distinction between those who have been to the mission field and those who have not. The only distinction He makes is between those who are following Him and those who are not.

A missionary is a "sent one." But whether at home or abroad, all Christians are to be continually aware of the Holy Spirit's leading. Some He may lead to stay at home, others He may lead to the mission field or to some other ministry.

What is important is that Christians are guided by Him. Therefore, a returning missionary must be very careful not to judge others because they are not on the mission field. Remember, it is not what you have done that counts; it is that your name is written in heaven with millions of other people God loves and calls His children. As Christians, we are all members of one another, and we cannot afford to judge each other's motives or calling.

Adjust to Change in Ministry

Resist the urge to impose the way you did things on the mission field onto the way you do things at home.

A year after leaving Youth With A Mission to return to hosting a television cooking show, Graham Kerr (the former Galloping Gourmet) wrote to tell us about his re-entry experience. He shared how he and his wife Treena had spent most of the first year trying to work in secular TV as though it were the mission field. He wrote:

> We attempted to use every subversive op-
> portunity to sow good seeds, and prayed

constantly to be good witnesses. Our hidden agenda clashed with the media.

After many, many months of pressured misunderstandings, we had a major break-through. By switching our commitment to being the best servants in our given task, and leaving the work of evangelism to the Holy Spirit's prompting within us, we have become far more effective both in our witness and in our commercial work.

In leaving the mission field to return home, you must adjust your methods to fit the new environment in which you find yourself. That does not mean you compromise your beliefs, but that you come to a place of balance, a place where you understand the different ways God would have you respond in various circumstances. Graham and Treena Kerr found that the secret to being effective Christians in their situation was to be good servants and to be prepared to follow the Holy Spirit's leading, and not to follow some formula of ministry that had worked in another situation.

Prepare for Reverse Culture Shock

Surprising as it may seem, some of the difficulty experienced by returning missionaries during re-entry is a result of their *success* on the mission field. Unfortunately, that success must be reversed when they return home. And what is their success? Cross-cultural adaptation. They have adapted so well to the culture in which they have been serving that they must undergo a reverse cultural adaptation back to their home culture.

My father spent over 40 years in China as a missionary. During that time, he had so adapted

to the Chinese culture that he experienced considerable difficulty relating to Western ways. A tele-
phone was an object of anxiety for him, and he
would invariably forget to hang up at the end of a
call. His idea of a sensible car was a Cadillac, since
a wealthy Christian man in the United States had
once given him a ride in his. When I was 24, my
dad said to me, "Peter, you should buy a Cadillac.
They're very comfortable!" Certainly. And very ex-
pensive! He had no idea of the relative value of
different commodities. But put my dad with the
Chinese, and he was right at home. He was never
happier than when he was trekking through the
"boonies" of China sharing the Gospel.

Cultural adaptation to the group you are serving with will happen, and the longer you are there,
the more it will occur. Unfortunately, many returning missionaries are unaware of just how
much they have adapted to the culture they have
been in, and return home thinking it will be easy
to readjust. But it is not, and they become victims
of reverse culture shock.

What are some of the signs of reverse culture
shock? One is *feeling "out of place*," as though you
are a spectator watching from afar. You don't really
fit in with what is going on around you. While
everyone else seems to be sure of their social
position, you seem to hang out at the edges, wanting to participate fully, but not being quite able to.

Another sign is *feeling lonely*. You feel isolated
from your closest friends and family members.
They have changed, and you don't always understand exactly where they're coming from. Thus you
feel like the "odd man out."

You may also find yourself *reacting in odd
ways*; weeping at a children's television program

or being completely overwhelmed by the number of television movies from which to choose on a typical Saturday night.

However, one of the biggest aspects of reverse culture shock is the *reaction to western material-ism.* Sometimes the material differences between what you have left on the mission field and that of your home culture are so jarring that you don't quite know how to react to them. Lance and Carol's experience illustrates what often happens.

Lance and Carol were missionaries to Brazil, where they ministered to street children. After two years of service in Brazil, they returned home to New York for Christmas. Their first evening home, they drove to a local mall to do some Christmas shopping. Carol had looked forward to this moment for a long time.

They stood together at the entrance to a large up-scale department store and stared. The sheer choice of products and the amount of people buying things overwhelmed them. Everything glittered and glowed, lights flashed on and off, numerous displays seemed to say, "buy me." They watched as people wandered aimlessly, wallets at the ready, looking for anything half-acceptable on which to spend their money. Carol saw one man take a $50 bill out of his pocket and buy a bottle of perfume without so much as looking to see what brand it was. She remembered Brazilian mothers who would give their souls for $50 worth of food to feed her children.

There just seemed too many choices and too much extravagance. Carol broke down and began to weep. As Lance helped her back to the car, she wondered how this had ever seemed normal to her.

Like Lance and Carol, many who have spent

time overseas, especially in less-developed areas, have been overwhelmed by the number of choices and the amount of waste in western nations. I know of returned missionaries who find it difficult to bring themselves to use a sprinkler to water their lawn, to use a tea bag only once, or to throw leftovers away, simply because they have seen the immense value of those items in other lands.

All of this takes time, but if you don't adjust in some measure to the "wasteful West," you will become critical of and alienated from others around you. You will find yourself becoming judgmental of your family and friends for doing exactly the same things you used to do. And as time goes by, you will find yourself falling back into those old habit patterns, and you will become angry and frustrated with yourself because of it.

The apostle Paul, who moved freely among a number of different cultures in the exercise of his ministry, had this to say on the subject: "I have learned to be content whatever the circumstances. I know what it is to be in need, and I know what it is to have plenty. I have learned the secret of being content in any and every situation, whether well fed or hungry, whether living in plenty or in want. I can do everything through him who gives me strength" (Philippians 4:11-13). Paul knew how to adapt to the circumstances in which he found himself. The returning missionary would do well to follow his example.

Re-entry is difficult, but not impossible to negotiate. Let's look at some practical things you can do to ease the stress you experience after your arrival home.

5

Back to Your Church

Ann had felt the strain in the relationship almost from the time Sherry stepped off the airplane. Sherry had been Ann's best friend, and Ann had looked forward with eager anticipation to the time when Sherry would return from her two years of missionary service in Chile. She missed the times of sharing together and encouraging one another in the Lord. But when Sherry arrived home, things were different.

God obviously had blessed Sherry's ministry among the poor people in the rural villages of Chile, and she had many wonderful stories to tell. But there was something else—an aloofness. It was as though Sherry looked down on Ann and anyone else who had not been to the mission field. Ann felt that she no longer measured up to Sherry's standard of spirituality, despite the wonderful things God had done in her life during Sherry's absence.

And Sherry seemed to be critical of everything. At church she pointed out people she called "pew-warmers." She berated the pastor for not confronting them with their lack of spirituality. One time, Sherry stood up in the weekly young adult's meet-

ing and asked why they were wasting their time
playing childish games when there was a world
outside dying in sin. She even accused Ann's
mother of being flippant in her relationship with
the Lord, because she chose to attend the local
garden circle meeting on Wednesday evenings
rather than the church prayer meeting.

At first, Ann had hoped all Sherry needed was
time to adjust back to life at home. But the passing
of time had only served to alienate Sherry further
from people. She had isolated herself from the rest
of the members of the church. It was as though
Sherry had never really left the mission field. She
wanted everything in church to be done just like
it had been done on the field. She wanted everyone
to adapt to her way of doing things, because she
felt that somehow it was better.

Ann tried to stay loyal to her friend, but it
became increasingly difficult. When they were out
together, Ann noticed how people avoided them.
Ann understood why; nobody wanted to be
dragged down by Sherry's constant criticism. She
wished she knew how to get through to Sherry and
make her see the way she was hurting and alien-
ating herself. She mused often over Sherry's problem. How could a person go from being a zealous
missionary to an obnoxious church critic in such
a short time? Why couldn't Sherry just fit in like
she had before?

Unfortunately, like Sherry, many returning
missionaries fail to make a clear distinction between the function of the mission organization and
the function of the local church. The mission organization takes a small number of committed
Christians and trains them to function as an "attack unit," piercing into new areas to share the

Gospel. The missions environment is a highly focused environment where those involved know God has called them to undertake a specific task, and they pour themselves into completing it.

By contrast, the local church is a broad, diverse, multifaceted entity. While the mission organization narrowly focuses on the task at hand, the local church sees missionary endeavor as one of a number of important tasks it is called to undertake. The local church sends and supports missionaries, but its focus is broader than that alone.

As a result of this broad focus, the local church is pulled in many directions. It must respond to people's needs on a variety of levels, be they spiritual, social, physical, economic, or even political. The church consists of people at various levels of emotional and spiritual maturity. Some are strong, mature Christians, while others are recent converts who are still struggling to bring areas of their lives under the lordship of Christ. And the church must embrace all these people and minister to them.

The leader of a missions organization has the prerogative of asking those who are spiritually or emotionally immature, or who do not fully support or flow in with the overall objectives of the mission, to leave. The local church pastor has no such prerogative. His charge is to love and encourage people in their relationship with God, no matter how weak or faltering they may be. The pastor cannot ask a person to leave the church simply because they are not a mature Christian. It is his job to lead them to new levels of maturity in Christ.

It is important for every returning missionary to understand this difference. The dynamics of the mission field are very different from those of the local church. To fail to make the distinction, as in Sherry's case, is to compare apples to oranges, which only leads to frustration and criticism.

Sherry's is not an isolated case. In talking with recently returned missionaries, I've found that they often make statements that reflect Sherry's sentiments. They say things like:

- My church really isn't interested in me.

- The church seems so out-of-focus, and the pastor is always too busy to talk.

- Nobody in the church understands me anymore.

- The pastor doesn't want to hear how we did things on the mission field.

- The pastor is not interested in talking with me about church problems I see.

- There's such a lack of spirituality in the church.

- People in my church are so materialistic.

- Worship times at church are so dull; they don't have the vibrancy of our worship times on the mission field.

- Prayer is a sometime thing.

The list could go on, but I think you get the picture. Many returning missionaries are frustrated by and critical of their local churches.

On the other hand, pastors are often frustrated with returning missionaries. When surveyed several years ago, pastors said:

- Returning missionaries expect to be served rather than to serve.

- Returning missionaries tend to have difficulty identifying with and fitting back into the congregation.

- Returning missionaries are too reliant on the "team" concept, and are at a loss without it.

- Returning missionaries tend to think the way they learned to do things on the mission field is superior to the way the church does things.

- Returning missionaries don't understand the way a church functions, nor the constraints under which a pastor must work.

- Returning missionaries tend to stay on the sidelines of church rather than to participate fully in church life.

- Returning missionaries tend to set unrealistically high standards for others in the congregation to measure up to.

- Returning missionaries can be very critical of things in the church.

- Returning missionaries want to be set loose to solve the problems of the church.

I am sure both perspectives have elements of truth, and that some of the criticisms of both are unwarranted or excessive. However, it shouldn't be like this at all. Returning missionaries should be a great blessing to their local church, not a hindrance and source of frustration. They should not be returning home to sit in judgment of their local church because it doesn't function at the same level of intensity as the mission organization in which they served. The fact is, it's not supposed to. Different dynamics are at play. A different "glue" holds the church together, and it is the job of every returning missionary to adjust to it. The responsibility is on the returning missionary to make every effort to ensure that they are a source of great blessing to their pastor and church.

Don't Be Critical

Tragically, many missionaries return home feeling as though their time away has earned them a certificate to criticize their church. This attitude is particularly prevalent among those who have been away as short-term missionaries. I suspect this is because the short-termer has really only experienced the "honeymoon" phase of missions, where everything seems exciting and new. They haven't been on the mission field long enough to see that both the mission organizations and the other missionaries have their own sets of problems to deal with. Because of this, short-term missionaries tend to come home thinking the situation on the mission field is wonderful, while things in their church are mired in the mundane.

Time spent on the mission field can be a positive, life-changing, character-transforming experience. However, such an experience does not mean that a missionary is more special than those in the church who have never been to the mission field. There are no grounds for returning missionaries to stand back and criticize their church. Such criticism is rooted in elitism and pride. Remember, God resists the proud, but gives grace to the humble (James 4:6).

A returning missionary should come home humble, not haughty. Resist the urge to compare and criticize, especially when you feel people don't understand you or what you have been through. Mature people are patient with immature people. If your experience on the mission field has matured you, it should work itself out in your life through *more* patience and *less* criticism. If that is not the case, ask yourself if you are as mature as you think you are.

Many missionaries who return home make the process of fitting back into their church difficult for themselves. They approach things with an attitude that stinks. They are proud, arrogant, and critical. They expect the church to adjust to them, instead of adjusting themselves to their church. In so doing, they neglect the example of Christ, who humbly adapted Himself to our world in order to enter it and minister life to people.

Much clamor is heard today as people criticize the Church. "The Church is too liberal. The Church is too worldly and materialistic. The Church has lost its vision for the lost. The Church is too political." The list goes on and on. Christian books, magazines, television, and radio, as well as the secular media, pour forth criticism of Christians and the Church. Some of it is justified.

However, what a pastor longs to hear is not another voice in the clamor, but someone who will say to him, "Pastor, I'm committed to this church. I'm committed to your leadership. I want to serve you and this body of believers. I'll do whatever needs to be done." Such an attitude avoids the pitfall of criticism which has tripped so many other returning missionaries. Remember, the battle is not with other people, but with spiritual powers

(Ephesians 6). When a situation at church dis-
tracts or irritates you, you have two choices: become critical and judgmental or become an
intercessor.

Be a Servant

One of the best ways I know to make the adjustment back to life in the local church is through
being a servant. Philippians 2:6-7 tells us that in
coming into our world, Christ took on the form of
a servant. The meaning of the words in the original
Greek make it very clear that Christ did not come
into the world pretending to be a servant, or as an
actor acting out the role of a servant. Rather, He
was a servant. Through and through, every ounce
of His being proclaimed that He was a servant.
When He served people, it flowed from who He was
at the core of His being.

As a returning missionary, you are leaving the
world of the mission field and re-entering the
world of your home culture and home church, and
servanthood is the model God wants you to follow.
From the core of your being, He wants you to reach
out and serve your church.

Unfortunately, many return from the mission
field having seen God use them in a certain way or
ministry, and expect to be used the same way in
their church upon their arrival home. When this
doesn't happen, they either demand it of the pastor or sit on the sidelines of the church and mope.
But that is not the way of the servant. Instead of
demanding, the servant asks what needs to be
done, and sets about doing it. Regardless of what
needs doing—be it cleaning the church toilets,
running the nursery during services, or teaching
a Sunday school class—the servant does it with a

joyful heart, and in obedience to the Lord.

This is not to say that you should give up all aspirations of being used in the particular ministry you feel God has gifted you in or called you to. It is simply recognizing that as a Christian, you are primarily a servant. It is your credential. It is what identifies you as Christ's. You bear His mark; in your very nature, you have become a servant, just as He did.

I alluded earlier to the fact that I was a jet pilot for the Royal Canadian Air Force for several years. If I were to apply today for another job as a pilot, my prospective employer would want to review my credentials. He would want to see that my pilot's license is up to date, that I have the proper educational qualifications, and he also would want a letter from the Air Force attesting to my skill as a pilot. And despite my past experience as an aviator, if my credentials are not in order or if they cast doubt upon my ability to handle the job, the prospective employer is not going to offer me the job.

It's the same for the returning missionary. You must first demonstrate to your church that your credentials as a Christian are in order. The best credential you can hold forth is your Christlikeness, which is ultimately best demonstrated through servanthood, since Christ was in essence a servant.

Proverbs 18:16 says, "A man's gift makes room for him and brings him before great men" (Amp.). As you serve joyfully in your church, the pastor, elders, and congregation will sense the sincerity of your heart. They will see that your credentials are in order, and they will provide opportunities for you to function in the ministry to which you feel God has called you.

Jesus offered a poignant warning when He spoke about men who attend a feast and presume themselves good enough to sit in the place of honor. How embarrassed they feel when someone else comes along and the host publicly relegates them to the bottom of the table in order to seat the new guest in the place of honor. "But when you are invited, take the lowest place, so that when your host comes, he will say to you, 'Friend, move up to a better place.' Then you will be honored in the presence of all your fellow guests. For everyone who exalts himself will be humbled, and he who humbles himself will be exalted" (Luke 14:10-11).

Serve joyfully in your local church in whatever capacity you are asked. Allow relationships and trust to develop to the point where your gifts begin to shine. Rather than pushing yourself forward, trust God to orchestrate events. Do not repeat the mistake of those men who assumed the place of honor, only to be publicly humiliated. Rather, humble yourself and serve, and in due course you will be raised up (James 4:10).

As with everything else, there is a balance here. Tragically, some churches tend to abuse those who offer to serve. If you feel your church is placing unreasonable demands upon you, don't think that the most "spiritual" thing to do is to endure it. You are responsible for your own well-being, so seek wider council. Allow mature Christians from outside your church or denomination to be a sounding board for your feelings. After talking with them, you may need to go to your pastor and sort the situation out. In extreme cases, it may be better to remove yourself from the church altogether.

Be Accountable to Others

You may have found yourself ministering in varied, interesting, or even difficult situations during your time on the mission field. For many, time spent on the mission field is also a time of great victory personally and spiritually. But don't let your experiences on the mission field give you an inflated idea about your own spiritual strength.

It is tragic, but true, that many Christians have experienced their greatest falls, spiritually and morally, after times of great personal victory; victory brings vulnerability with it. This is when many Christians let down their guard and reap devastating consequences. Don't be lulled into letting down your guard when you return home. Don't say to yourself, *I've become strong as a result of my time on the mission field. I can handle things.* You are not strong, and you cannot handle things alone. You are not superhuman. You are not immune to life's temptations.

The apostle Paul has a warning for people who think otherwise: "For by the grace given me I say to every one of you: Do not think of yourself more highly than you ought, but rather think of yourself with sober judgment, in accordance with the measure of faith God has given you" (Romans 12:3). And in I Corinthians 10:12-13: "If you think you are standing firm, be careful that you don't fall! No temptation has seized you except what is common to man. And God is faithful; he will not let you be tempted beyond what you can bear. But when you are tempted, he will also provide a way out so that you can stand under it."

What is the way out God provides? I believe it is accountability. It is holding yourself open before others; sharing your emotions, your temptations, and your weaknesses; and asking these friends to help you bear them. It is asking your friends to hold you to account in all areas of your life so you do not cave in to temptation.

I received the following letter from a young person who had served for several years on the mission field and then returned home. Tragically, it illustrates all too well what I have been saying:

> I'd served [as a missionary] in another culture for several wonderful, hard years— some of those years as a leader. It was time to come home for a while, yet I really didn't know the "where" and "when" of my return to missions.

> It was good to be home. Yet somehow I didn't fit. I felt awkward in all situations— family, job, even church. I wasn't sure what was expected of me. So instead of talking to someone, I tried to live up to what I thought were people's expectations of me as a "Christian"...[and] a "missionary."

> I wanted so much to tell people, "Hey, I'm struggling; I feel like I don't belong. I don't know what's expected of me." But pride kept me from sharing what was really in my heart. After all I *knew* the answers, had even counseled others. But just knowing the answers didn't help.

> So the test came. God was asking me to totally trust Him with a relationship. It seemed like He was asking me to lay it down. I found myself on very shaky ground. I clung to whatever comfort I could get. In spite of

all my "knowledge" of what to do, I made a definite, conscious choice. I fell into the sin of immorality.

There was a morning when I woke up and felt so empty inside, and so cold, inside and out. I sensed there were demons surrounding me, laughing at my devastation. I knew I had to run back to God and ask His forgiveness.

But even after deeply repenting...I still felt God could not love me anymore. How could I deliberately walk away from Him? I was forgiven, but could He ever trust me again? Would I ever regain my closeness to Him?

The hardest thing was to forgive myself. I had failed God and all those who had believed in me and supported me in missions. Finally, in desperation, I confessed to my pastor and others I trusted. What I received through them was God's love for me. Then, and only then, was I able to look in the mirror and forgive myself.

Since then, I have drawn much closer to the Lord. His words are gentle now, and I can hide in the shelter of His wings....But I must walk in the truth I know, and constantly be on guard. I am still hurt, but I am healing.

There is great safety in accountability. I'm sure that no Christian determines to fall into immorality, or any other sin for that matter. You can avoid it. After you arrive home, draw together a group of godly men and women from your church and hold yourself accountable to them. Be humble and open to their input into your life, not just in the area of resisting temptation, but in adjusting to life back in your church. Accountability is God's basis for support, so hold fast to it.

Reach out to People

While you may expect people to be interested in hearing about your experiences on the mission field, don't be disappointed if that doesn't happen. Upon your return, expect to encounter a varied range of attitudes from people in your church toward you. Some will be interested in everything you did on the mission field. Some will ridicule you as though you have been away at some exotic location on a vacation. Others will write you off as crazy for going at all. Some will simply be indifferent, and not really care where you went and what you did.

Whatever the attitude you encounter, don't allow it to offend you and cause you to withdraw into emotional and social hibernation. Rather, reach out to people. If they don't seem interested in what you did during your time away, become interested in them. Ask questions about their life. What have they been doing during your time away? How is their family? How is their business? Respond to them in the opposite spirit. Be interested in them. Love them. Tell them how good it is to see them again.

Above all, don't sit around and bemoan how misunderstood you feel, and how uncaring people are toward you. This may be true, but your positive reaction to them is far more important to God. His desire is that you have a positive re-entry experience, and avoid dropping into the pit of despair.

Some Practical Matters

Listed below are some practical points to remember as you re-enter your home church and begin making the adjustment to life there.

Arrange to Meet with the Pastor First

Many returning missionaries flunk the test right here. They expect the pastor to initiate a meeting with them, and when he doesn't, they never recover. Don't let it happen to you. Initiate a meeting with your pastor. Call him, find a convenient time in his schedule, and arrange to visit him. And remember to take the small gift you brought home for him.

At the meeting, greet the pastor and give him a brief review of where you went and why (if he is not already familiar with this). During your time of sharing, be sure to include:

- What the Lord did in your life while you were away.

- The things God used to bring about these changes.

- Suggestions of ways you would like to share with the church about your experiences (e.g., a slide presentation for Sunday school or Wednesday evening Bible study). Be specific.

- Answers to your pastor's questions.

- Reiteration of your continued submission to his authority, welcoming his continued input into your life. (If you have not submitted to him and welcomed his input in the past, make that right first!)

- Ask him if there are any areas of the
  church where more help is needed, and be
  prepared to fill in wherever you are
  needed, be it the cleaning roster or
  mowing the church lawns.

Remember that the pastor is a busy man, so keep your meeting brief and respectful, unless he indicates that he would like to hear more. It's better to be asked to continue rather than be ushered out the door still talking!

Be sure you do not criticize or compare your missions experience to the local church in any way. The last thing a pastor wants to hear is, "I can see a real weakness in the church in worship. If I were the worship leader, I wouldn't do things that way. I think it would be much better done this way." If that is your attitude, I can guarantee that your pastor will not let you anywhere near the worship leader. So even if you are convinced you're right (and there would be some doubt about that!), bite your tongue and say nothing.

As your meeting with the pastor draws to a close, go over any specific plans you may have made together. For example, "I will wait for you to talk to the Sunday School Director, then I will call him on Thursday about the details of my presentation." Do not leave room for misunderstanding.

Thank Your Supporters

Be sure you thank those who have supported you through prayer or finances while you were on the mission field. Again, you take the initiative.

I received a letter recently from an older lady who wrote: "Five years ago, I returned home from teaching at a Bible school in Malaysia. There was absolutely no welcome or interest from my church. One elder said, 'Welcome home' as he shook my hand at the door, and that was about it. Even though I had been on a church-approved and sponsored project, I was not given any opportunity to thank the church for their support, nor to report back to them on what had happened. To this day, I never have had the opportunity to share."

Let's be real! This person has stewed away for five years over the fact that she was never invited to speak to the church and thank them for their support. Why didn't she take the initiative? She could have invited those who were interested in what she had been doing in Malaysia over for a meal after church on Sunday. In that context, she could have thanked people for their support, shared with them about what she had done while she was away, and answered any questions. How sad that this woman still remembers her home-coming with bitterness five years later. It has held her in bondage; it didn't have to, if she had taken the initiative.

Seek Other Avenues to Share Your Experiences

There are many other places apart from a Sunday morning service where you may be able to share about your mission experiences. What about the monthly men's or women's meetings? There may be a regular prayer breakfast or early morning prayer meeting at which you could share. There is also Sunday school, both the adult and children's classes. You may also be able to speak at a local Christian school, or to a children's club.

Following are a few guidelines to remember as you prepare to speak.

• Make sure you know exactly how long you

are expected to speak, and don't go over
that time. It is a good idea to have a
rehearsal beforehand and time yourself.

- Start with a humorous anecdote about
  some aspect of your time away, or some
  embarrassing language faux pas. This
  serves to get the audience "with you." Just
  make sure the humor is at *your* expense,
  not someone else's!

- Pick out one theme, and stick to it
  throughout your presentation. For
  example, you may choose to talk about
  God's call to Abraham, and how he was
  blessed in order that he could be a
  blessing to others (Genesis 22:17-18).
  From this, you could talk about the ways
  you can see that God has blessed you and
  your culture. You could then go on to tell
  of the various ways in which you saw that
  blessing being transferred to those with
  whom you were working. Perhaps you
  could share how your Sunday school
  training as a child laid the foundation for
  you to be able to conduct Bible studies on
  the mission field, and see people commit
  their lives to Christ as a result. Or how
  your nursing training allowed you to bring
  relief to hurting children in a slum. Or
  how your role as a support worker
  contributed to the overall success of a
  mission project or team. The idea is to
  arrange the stories of your experiences

into a cohesive framework, if possible
relating back to home and church instead
of simply telling them in disjointed bits.
Finish your presentation by repeating
your theme Scripture.

- Leave some time at the end for questions.

- If at all possible, set up a display for
people to look at after your presentation,
and be near your display to answer any
further questions people may have.

- The next day, write a thank-you note to
the person who arranged the meeting.

If someone asked your pastor how well you
fitted back into the church, how would he reply? I
hope he would not be led to make any of the
negative comments about you that were recorded
earlier in this chapter. Rather, I pray that he would
say that you serve diligently, are a person of humility who doesn't criticize, take a vital interest in
the welfare of the church, and pray for the church.
May he be so impressed by your spirit and attitude
that he becomes eager to see others from the
church released into missions in order to reap the
benefits in their lives that you have reaped in
yours. May it be so.

6

Horror Stories

Part of the process of fitting back into the local church and into the broader community of Christians is reestablishing relationship links with various individuals. In the course of this, you may encounter some surprising or even hurtful responses.

People do not always respond the way you would like them to. When you think they will be sympathetic to you, they prove to be unsympathetic. When you think they will understand, they do not. Many returned missionaries have horror stories to tell of their treatment at the hands of Christians upon their return home.

This chapter contains several of these stories in the hope that by reading them, you will be prepared for some of the responses you may encounter upon your return home. They are extreme cases, but they illustrate the bizarre nature of some of the situations you could face. As you read these true accounts, try to put yourself in the place of the returning missionaries involved. Ask yourself how you would react in each situation. Look for ways the difficulties could have been alleviated, diverted, or perhaps even avoided.

Misunderstanding

Andrea, a missionary in her early thirties, had been through a mission training school, and had spent seven years serving in Asia. She was a wonderful secretary who organized the office of the national mission agency director. She welcomed people, wrote schedules, coped with all the office correspondence, arranged meetings, and was a wonderful, gracious witness in all she did. The local people loved her, and it was easy to see that she had found her niche.

Andrea was home on furlough when her pastor and church elders called her in for an interview. At the interview, they suggested that Andrea was not "properly trained" to carry out her job because she had not attended the denomination's Bible college. They said she was not strong enough theologically, and therefore could not be an effective missionary. Because of this, the elders did not want her to return to the mission field, and they said that the church would not support her financially or spiritually if she chose to do so against their wishes.

Devastated by this turn of events, Andrea sought my help. I called the leader of the mission she had served with to verify her situation. He was enthusiastic in his praise of Andrea. So we set up a meeting with the leaders of the church.

The meeting proved fruitless. The elders had virtually no overseas exposure. Only one had ever been out of the country, and then only to Costa Rica to spend two weeks in a luxury condominium. None had seen Andrea at work or had any real idea of what she did on the mission field. I explained how valuable she was to her mission, and how perfectly she was suited to the work. But it was to no avail. Despite Andrea's proficiency and value on the mission field, these men had decided she needed a degree from the denominational Bible school to be a truly effective missionary. They had made up their minds, and would not be dissuaded.

Naturally, Andrea felt hurt and totally misunderstood. For seven years, she had served as a missionary; she knew God had called her. She had been efficient at her job, and was effective in her ministry, seeing a number of people come to know Christ. Now she was being told that because she didn't have a Bible college degree, all her work on the mission field had been negated. She was no longer an effective missionary, and wouldn't be until she got a degree. And all of this from a group of men who had never even visited the mission field. Andrea wept uncontrollably.

My heart broke for her. Yet despite how she felt, I counseled Andrea that there was only one response she could have toward the elders—forgiveness. To do anything less than forgive would be to invite anger and bitterness into her life, and would cause her to unrighteously judge the elders of her church. It was not an easy test for Andrea to pass, but she persevered and came to the place where she could forgive.

After spending several years developing other avenues of sponsorship and support, Andrea was finally able to return to Asia.

Hostility

After three years on the mission field, Larry and Fran and their four-year-old daughter returned home for a six-month furlough. They had been serving with an interdenominational mission, although their own denomination had a strong missionary arm. As a result, they had never asked for nor received any financial support from their home church. When they left for the mission field, they had only $20 a month in pledged support. But God had been faithful, providing enough money from other sources for them to be able to meet their living costs and to take a furlough.

Shortly after arriving home, the church mission board asked Larry and Fran to share with them about their ministry on the mission field. Larry and Fran were very excited about this, as it was the first official recognition they had received from their church. They were enthusiastic and optimistic as they headed off for the meeting. It did not take long, however, for their enthusiasm and optimism to drain away as they began to see the true motives of several on the mission board.

The members of the board began asking very specific questions about Larry and Fran's finances, which they answered honestly. As the meeting progressed, two of the older board members became hostile toward the young couple, scrutinizing closely every facet of their ministry on the mission field. It was as though they had become their accusers, asking such barbed questions as: "Larry, how could you be so irresponsible in taking your family to the mission field the way you did? What would you have done if one of you had become ill? And why would you choose to go and serve with an interdenominational mission agency when our denomination has a perfectly good missions agency of its own?"

By the time the meeting drew to a close, Fran could barely hold back her tears. She and Larry felt violated; their credibility had been attacked

and undermined. They were stunned at the way
the mission board had failed to even acknowledge
the ways God had blessed and provided for them
over the past three years. The fact that Larry and
Fran had tried to "walk by faith" seemed a terrible
crime to them. That they had succeeded seemed to
incense some members of the mission board.

Larry and Fran recovered from the shock of the
meeting. In their hearts they knew they had to
forgive the members of the mission board. It wasn't
easy, but they did it. As a result of their right
response to the situation, and because of their
faithful service on the mission field during the
previous three years, they were able to significantly increase their level of monthly support before returning. The leader of the mission agency in
the nation Larry and Fran had been serving wrote
a letter, praising them and their work. This so
impressed their pastor that he ignored the mission
board's negative recommendation, and committed
the church to monthly financial support of Larry
and Fran.

Apathy

Sarah was a nurse from Kansas City who spent
six months with a short-term medical outreach
team in the Philippines. The team worked with a
community of about 5,000 people who had made
their home atop Manila's garbage dump at a place
called Balut.

Sarah came from a sheltered life in the mid-
west, and she saw sights that shook her to the
core. She watched fly-covered children raking
through piles of newly deposited garbage from the
city, looking for anything worth salvaging and
selling. She ministered to the people in dilapidated

shacks made from materials scrounged from the dump. She watched mothers prepare food for their families amid the stench of decaying trash. She saw people lie down and sleep right on top of the garbage. In the dry season, spontaneous combustion turned the dump into a smoke-belching incarnation of hell. In the wet season, it became a knee-deep sea of putrid mud. And swarming flies were everywhere.

On one occasion, Sarah's medical team found the bloated bodies of two men tied to a bridge pier in the most polluted water Sarah had ever encountered. The team members stood chest deep in jet-black, rancid water, their feet sinking into the gooey river bottom, as they cut the bodies loose. The two men had been murdered, both shot in the head. But no one really cared. No police came to investigate. Some even indicated that the police had probably done the killing.

It was all part of life on the dump, and it had changed Sarah profoundly. After getting over the initial shock of Balut, she had found new reservoirs of inner strength to draw upon to keep going. She had learned much about herself and about the world. She had also experienced a new depth in her relationship with the Lord.

When Sarah arrived home, she was brimming with news of what she had experienced. She couldn't wait to tell her friends and family. But people weren't interested. There were the superficial, cursory questions: "What was the food like? Did you get eaten by bugs? Did you see any snakes? Was it hot and sticky where you lived? Did you have air conditioning?" But no one seemed that much interested in what she had been doing, what she had experienced, and how it had affected her. No one asked in-depth and probing questions, the kind of questions Sarah was eager to answer. Sarah was saddened and hurt by the apathy she encountered, especially that of other Christians, from whom she had expected more.

Understanding Apathy

Perhaps the most common reaction from people toward returning missionaries is indifference and apathy. People do not seem to have any real interest in what the returning missionary has seen and done. They may ask questions, but they are usually superficial ones, more closely aligned to decorum and politeness than they are to a genuine interest in the returning missionary's experiences. Members of the returning missionary's church and family are not immune from this.

Why do people, especially other Christians whom we thought would be understanding and interested, respond with such indifference? Following are several reasons for this apathy. Although there is no surefire way of dealing with apathy, understanding it may help us bear it.

Information Overload

Usually, people don't intentionally mean to be indifferent or apathetic toward returning missionaries. Instead, their apathy grows from their changed perception of the world, which in turn means a changed perception of what missionaries do. When William Carey left for India, or Dr. Livingston for Africa, they were going to exotic, unexplored continents filled with strange landscapes, animals, and people. There was a mystique, a romance about what they were setting out to do.

But today, through the wizardry of electronics,

most of that mystique and romance has dissipated. Africa and India are beamed into our living rooms daily. Their images dance across our television screens, unveiling the secrets of life in other places. Right now, as famine haunts East Africa, our televisions take us there. We can experience the sights and sounds of that famine. We can hear the cry of hungry children, the wail of a mother for her child that has starved to death, and see the desperation in the eyes of a man who can no longer feed his family. And we can stop to talk about the situation with the U.N. workers seeking to alleviate the suffering.

And not just Africa...every continent, every nation, is beamed into our home in the course of a day, a week, a month, a year. As a result, places which once were exotic and mysterious have now become commonplace. People's perceptions of the world change. Microwave beams bouncing from television transmitters to satellites to our homes have shrunk the world. Those far-off places where missionaries go to serve seem almost as though they are in the neighbor's backyard.

The result of this changed perception of the world is often apathy. *Compassion burnout* is a term in common use today. Ask anyone from an aid organization dependent upon the general public for its support, and they will tell you what the term means. Disasters, devastation, wars, and famine have become so common as we watch them on television that people have become indifferent and apathetic toward those events. Overloaded with all the gory sensory detail of the latest horror, people retreat into apathy as a means of escape. So we should not be surprised that people have a similar reaction to missionaries who come bearing graphic tales of what they have seen and done.

Real changes in the world have also changed people's perceptions of missions. I remember reading Brother Andrew's book, *God's Smuggler*, and marveling at what he was doing. How courageous he was, trusting God to blind the eyes of Soviet border guards as he ferried vanloads of Bibles into their country. But now truckloads of Bibles are taken into the former Soviet Union without fear of punishment. It doesn't make what Brother Andrew did any less courageous; it has simply changed our perception of missions in the former Soviet Union. To minister today in Russia or Eastern Europe is no big deal. People take vacations there! It doesn't mean that the work missionaries are doing in the former Eastern Bloc countries is less important than what Brother Andrew did. It's just different, and because of changed perceptions, it now seems more mundane.

Family, friends, and other Christians don't necessarily mean to be indifferent or apathetic toward you; it's just that going to the other side of the world to share the Gospel is not such a major undertaking anymore. People fly halfway around the world just to take a vacation these days. So if you don't get asked a lot of questions about what it was like serving on the mission field, it is often because many people already think they know; they've seen it on TV.

Difficulty in Relating to Missionaries

Few Christians, much less non-Christians, really understand what motivates missionaries or how to relate to them. Somehow, many in the church have a stereotypical, caricatured view of missionaries. They think that missionaries are oddballs or freaks of nature who can't make it in the real world. Their clothes never fit right, and they are terminally boring people. All they can think about and talk about is missions. They seem impervious to many of life's enjoyments like football, baseball, a day at the beach, or a night at the movies. They can't seem to make it on their own in the real world, so they retreat to the mission field. This is the Protestant equivalent of the equally stereotypical view of people who become nuns or join monastic orders.

With such a distorted view, is it any wonder that some people find it difficult to know how to relate to a missionary? They don't really know what makes a missionary "tick," so they tend to stay on the safe ground of keeping conversations vague. The last thing they want to do is to push the missionary's button and get him talking ad infinitum about missions. Most people's concentration span on a single topic is about three minutes, so no one wants to risk having to endure a thirty-minute verbal deluge about missions.

To overcome this perception, make sure you never tell a person more than they appear interested in knowing. As you talk, stop and ask the person if they would like to hear about a certain aspect of what you did. If they say they are too busy or not interested, don't push it. Better to have a person ask you to go on than to have someone trying to politely escape your company.

Then there are those people who are interested in hearing more of what you did on the mission field, but because of their preconceived notions about missionaries, they don't know how to start a meaningful conversation with you. They know they want to talk to you, but all they can think of are dumb, dead-end questions to ask.

If you sense the person wants to know more, but is a little unsure of what to ask or how to proceed, you might try some creative answers to their questions. If they ask you what the food was like, you could answer something like this: "Well, it was very different. The preparation for breakfast started at 4 a.m. I would get up with the women of the house and begin collecting sticks for the fire...." Watch the person's face to see if his interest has been piqued, and if he wants to hear more. As you answer in this way, you can gently lead into a discussion of other subjects related to the mission field or on being a missionary.

Don't forget to talk to children about your missionary experiences. They love to hear stories, and will ask questions that many adults would like to, but don't. I can still remember the thrill of hearing missionaries' stories when I was a child—they made God sound so real.

Guilt

It is estimated that only five percent of those who say they have received a "call to missions" actually make it to the mission field. The other ninety-five percent get sidetracked in some way. Have you ever considered that some of your friends and family may be a part of that ninety-five percent who didn't make it? It is quite possible that you, a returning missionary, will evoke feelings of guilt in Christians who have felt called themselves, but never went.

When you come home excited and enthusiastic about missions, they are not going to be eager to hear you out. You will stir too many old feelings. You create a tension in them—an ambivalence. On the one hand, they are excited that you have followed through on your call to missions. They know the need; they have felt the call themselves. On the other hand, your presence disturbs them, because you summon to the surface the remembrance of their failure to follow the call of God to the mission field. So these Christians, too, would rather stick to surface, peripheral issues in any conversation with you. They admire you from a distance, but they are also leery of you; you make them feel guilty.

I know this is true, because I was like that. Although I was born into a missionary family, or perhaps because of it, I had a strong resistance to missionaries for many years. Privately, I held most of them in contempt. It was not until after I had totally surrendered to the lordship of Christ that I was at all open to becoming one myself!

Reestablishing relationships with people after your return from the mission field is not always easy. You are often at the mercy of other people's responses to you. And for some reason, nothing seems to stir up such mixed emotions in a person as does a missionary. So be on guard; don't let other people's responses rob you of your relationship with the Lord. Forgive much, love much, and walk humbly. By so doing, you will head off any condemnation that would seek to overtake you as a result of other people's reactions to you. Trust God, expect the best of people, and through your endurance, God will work steel into your spirit.

7

Families and Re-Entry

Single missionaries often view missionary families as the blessed ones. When a family leaves the mission field, they enjoy many advantages. If the family has learned a foreign language, there will always be someone with whom to practice the language, so they can stay fluent. The family members will also always have someone around who understands what they have been through and who has the same memories. And it is true, families do not normally feel as isolated and alienated as singles when they return home, because they have each other.

But returning missionary families have their own special set of stresses to face in the re-entry process. Parents who have their own re-entry experience with which to deal must also guide their children through it. And since people tend to react quite differently to similar circumstances, families often find themselves being pulled in opposite directions as a result of the re-entry stress placed upon them.

Because of the uniqueness of the stress encountered by families during re-entry, I have devoted an entire chapter to their situation.

Before You Leave the Mission Field

Parents need much wisdom in preparing to bring their children home from the mission field. Perhaps the most important thing you can do for your children is to talk to them about what to expect upon arrival home. Explain to them the things that will be different from the culture they are currently in, and what things will be the same. Your children have shorter memories than you do. In the space of two years, they may have forgotten much about their home country. Some may have been born on the mission field, and have never lived in their home country at all. It is also a good idea to get out the family photo album and start reintroducing your children to their grandparents, uncles, aunts, cousins, and family friends.

The lack of this preparation in my own re-entry experience was particularly devastating. While in the concentration camp in China, my mother had become ill with cancer, and had an operation as soon as she was released. Because of the general level of trauma in our family, and the lack of psychology applied to children in those days, I do not remember any preparation before my "transplanting" back to England. When we arrived "home," my mother was too ill to care for me, so I was shipped off to stay with an aunt and uncle and their two children. I was separated from my sick mother, my brothers, and my father, and was expected to adjust to English culture, food, and school; all with a family I had never met before! It took me years to get over it.

Psychologists say it is best to take as many of a child's special things as possible to give them a sense of stability. They do not say *how* to pack them! There are constraints, especially if you are traveling by airplane, and you simply can't take everything your children want to have along. The following are some general principles to follow:

Take Treasures Home

Allow your children to choose at least some of their special things to take home. There are those things which it is hard for a parent to believe any child could treasure. If children do treasure odd things, respect their choices. Moving time is not the right time to challenge a child's sense of the aesthetic. Also, allow your children to select gifts to take home to meaningful people in their lives.

Make Photo Albums

Take as many photos as possible of your children going about their normal daily routine and interacting with a variety of other people. Put these photographs in an album for your children, and allow them to show others their own record of missionary life. Write brief captions for the photographs if you have the time, recording the names of the people and places in them. Make a separate album for each of your children, as they each need to feel the uniqueness of their own experience on the mission field. I guarantee your children will still have these albums twenty years from now.

Break In New Things

Begin to get your children used to the things they will have with them when they arrive home. This is particularly important with small children. Get them accustomed to any new equipment. If, for example, you have bought a traveling crib or a folding baby seat to take home, start using it before you leave. In this way, no matter where you

are, your children will have the security of sleeping
or eating with familiar things. You may also want
to take your toddler's own eating bowl or special
silverware with you when you go. These things do
not take up much room, and they give a small child
a sense of continuity and security.

Conversely, do not wait until the day you leave
to discard your child's favorite toy or stuffed ani-
mal. Such an action is likely to cause a major
trauma in the home!

Begin to eliminate things you are not going to
be able to take home several weeks before you
leave. Go through your child's things, and put
aside what they will not be able to take with them.
Hopefully, this will lessen the impact of finally
having to leave these things. Of course, you will
want to temper this process with what was said
before.

Take Examples of School Work

If you have school-aged children, make sure
you bring home adequate examples of their school
work. Ask their teacher to provide a detailed list of
what they have accomplished in each area. This
will help in correct class placement in the future.
Also, once you get home, be sure to introduce
yourself to your child's new teacher. Arrange to
visit or phone once a week to discuss any problems
in curriculum or behavior until you both agree this
is no longer necessary. Each education system
arranges its curriculum differently, so chances are
your child will be ahead of his or her class in some
areas, and behind in others. Showing an interest
in your child's education will give the teacher the
incentive she needs to bring your child up to speed
in the areas in which he or she is behind.

Prepare for Culture Shock

Try to begin some "re-culturation" with your children before you get home. Think of the things your children do or say which may make them seem odd to your family and friends at home.

Susan and Rob had spent four years ministering in Taiwan. Their children Alice and Bobby were three and five years old, respectively, when they left Canada. As a result, Alice and Bobby remembered little about their birthplace; Taiwan was what they really knew as home. They spoke the language better than their parents, and had even begun to speak English with an accent. They loved Chinese food, and always ate with chopsticks.

Three months before they left for home, Susan and Rob decided it was time to start some re-culturation with their children. They named one night a week "Canada Night." Susan made the effort to find and cook foods that were common at home—steak, potatoes, dessert—things Grandma was sure to give the family to eat upon their arrival home. The children soon became accustomed to eating such foods.

The bigger challenge for the children, though, was learning to eat with a knife and fork. They found it awkward at first, but as the weeks went by, they became adept. In addition, Susan and Rob told Alice and Bobby about the things they remembered from their childhood in Canada, showing them picture books and photos. They also spent time explaining some of the differences between Taiwan and Canada.

When the family finally arrived home, Susan and Rob were glad about the preparation they had put into their children's re-entry. The kids still had strange accents, which the grandparents had difficulty accepting, but at least they had good table manners, which made up for a lot in Grandma's eyes. The time and effort they had put in to try and re-culturate their children back to Canada had really helped the children in their adjustment.

Debrief the Children

Don't forget to include your children in the debriefing process, especially if they are teenagers. Make sure they are included in any commissioning prayers before you leave.

Always remember that your children will feel secure as long as Mom and Dad are secure!

Arrival Home

It is best to try and keep some type of routine after you return home. The smaller the child is, the more important this becomes. Keeping a routine won't be easy initially, as there will be many demands on your time, and most likely a lot of traveling. But bear in mind that the more continuity a child feels, the happier they will be through this time of change. So if you had a family routine before you left the mission field, don't throw it out after you arrive home. Perhaps the best study I have read on this whole topic of continuity is in the book *What is a Family?* by Edith Schaeffer.[2] You may wish to read this book before you leave for home. It is well worth the effort.

Remember that a person can be very familiar to you, yet a stranger to your children. Try to let your children warm up to people in their own way. Grandma may have waited three years to meet little Johnny, but that does not mean little Johnny is ready to return her pent-up love. He may not want to be hugged to death and smothered with kisses from an old lady he has never seen before.

So be sensitive to your children. Don't force them upon people who may be strangers in their eyes. Also, while you'll probably be very busy speaking in churches or visiting with old friends upon your arrival home, be sensitive to how often you leave your children with a babysitter. When they first arrive home, you will probably be the only person familiar to them. As much as possible, allow them to dictate the speed at which they can cope with their expanding world. Be there for them to talk things over.

Change in Family Structure

There will be inevitable changes in your family as you return home. Some will be welcome changes; others will bring a sense of loss with them.

Warren and Kathy were American missionaries serving in East Africa. Warren was the principal of his denomination's small regional Bible college, while Kathy used her nurse's training to run a clinic for the local children. Warren and Kathy had three children whom they home-schooled. As part of the children's home-schooling curriculum, they participated in various aspects of their parents' ministry. For example, their older daughter, who was studying eleventh grade accounting, helped Warren keep the Bible college's books in order; their twelve-year-old son was in charge of keeping track of the inventory in the clinic; and their ten-year-old made posters related to various health issues, aimed at parents who brought their children to the clinic.

The time came when Warren and Kathy felt they
needed to take their children home, particularly to
prepare their older daughter for college. Three
months after arriving home, they were still reeling
from all that was happening.

Warren had been asked to speak at many
churches and Bible colleges, so he spent much of
his time traveling to fulfill those engagements. On
the other hand, Kathy, who had been such an
integral part of their ministry on the mission field,
felt as though no one took her seriously any more.
To most people, she was simply "Warren's wife."
Back in Africa, she had handled a high level of
responsibility and ministry. She felt frustrated
that she never got invited to speak. To make matters worse, since they had little money to put their
daughter through college, Kathy had to take a job
as a part-time nurse at a local hospital.

Their daughter loved her new school, and she
seemed to want to make up for all the electives she
had missed throughout her life on the mission
field. She was on the volleyball team, in the drama
club, and was a cheerleader. She was constantly
busy with extracurricular activities, which, of
course, cost extra money.

The two younger children were instantly ad-
dicted to television, a questionable luxury with
which they hadn't had to contend in Africa. These
two did not want to do any more than the bare
minimum of chores around the house.

When Warren and Kathy finally sat down to
discuss the situation, they both expressed a sense
of grief at the changes that had occurred in their
previously close-knit family. Everyone seemed to
be going in opposite directions; no one had the
time or energy anymore to be involved with each

other's projects. How different life in Africa had been! With few distractions, no television, and little outside entertainment, it had been easy to stay close as a family—they had been a team. Life back home was far more complicated, and took much more planning than Warren and Kathy had ever imagined.

Part of Warren and Kathy's story was inevitable; all returning missionary families will be challenged in similar ways. If your family is focused and close-knit while on the mission field, you will experience a degree of grief upon returning home, as family members find new interests and friends. You will encounter parents and in-laws again, and will have to adjust to the demands of having an extended family around. And as if that is not enough, each family member will be experiencing their own level of re-entry stress, trying to deal with it in their own way. The ensuing state of flux can lead to some stretching times!

Be prepared. Make sure you keep an atmosphere in the family where everyone feels they can talk openly about their feelings. The environment should always be non-threatening and accepting.

Helping Your Teenagers Through

You should try to see re-entry through the eyes of your teenagers. More than anything else, teenagers want to blend in. They are often embarrassed by the things that single them out as different from others. Because of this, parents must be very sensitive to the feelings and needs of their teenaged children.

At a time in his life when it is important that he feels like part of the group, your returning teenager is obviously going to stick out. As a result, he is likely to be nervous about fitting back in, and may be very sensitive to things which are not important to you as an adult. If you have a teenager, discuss with him exactly what you expect of him in various situations.

Resist the urge to put your children (particularly teenagers) on show. Teenagers do not like to be put on the spot, so if you are asked to speak or give a presentation of your work at a church, be sure to let them know ahead of time if you want them to join in. If you call your teenager to the front of the church to sing without checking with him first, you are asking for major trouble!

Wherever possible, try to give your teenager as much leeway as possible. Take the matter of clothes, for example. Depending on where you served, teenage fashions will likely have changed since you left for the mission field. Have someone who is familiar with teenage fashions go shopping with you and your teenager. Let them guide you in what to buy, since clothing is one important way teens can feel that they fit in with their peers.

Teenagers are also sensitive about having their friends over to visit. If their friends do come, make every effort to be sensitive to them. Don't embarrass your child by talking to his or her friend in a foreign language, telling missionary stories, or reminding their friend what a different upbringing your child has had.

If your teenager gets frustrated or even angry with you, don't worry. He's not in the process of backsliding; he's just at a point in his life where fitting in with other teens is important As a developing young adult, he is simply trying to find out where he belongs in the world, and you must give him the room he needs to find that place.

Researchers have also found that many teenagers who grow up overseas, then re-enter their culture, often experience delayed adolescence. This is particularly true of teenagers from westernized countries. This delayed adolescence has been recorded in people up to the age of twenty-two years. Often the host culture they grew up in was so structured that by all appearances, these young people seemed to have a very easy time of adolescence. There was no rebellion, and no significant questioning of authority. However, the real truth could be that they have yet to face the choices and decisions that make adolescence such a tumultuous time for the western teenager.

The best way to help your teenager through the re-entry process is by being quietly supportive. Let him know that he can talk to you about *anything* that is troubling him, and that you are there to make the re-entry as easy for him as possible.

Your family is the greatest possession God will ever entrust to you. Re-entry is one of the greatest challenges your family will face. Your job as a parent is to help your children through the adjustment to life at home. This does not mean it will be easy for them, but you are there when they need you. You are available to pray with them, talk with them, listen to their fears and frustrations, and offer any insights and help you might have. Your family's well-being should be very important to you, and your family can be strengthened through adversity.

As a parent, you will struggle through re-entry yourself as you guide your children through it. It won't be easy. Some days, the pressure will feel unbearable. You will feel like "unloading" on your children. You will wonder if going to the mission field was worth it after all.

These are very normal feelings. When confronted with the same situation, most people would feel the same way. But Christians have a loving heavenly Father who wants us to lean on Him through the process. If the going gets so tough that it seems unbearable, take time out to seek God. Gather your children, and lay your cares, concerns, fears, failures, and frailties before Him.

He is faithful. His word and the experience of His people through the ages attest to that fact. You do not need to bear the burden of re-entry for yourself and your family alone. How tragic it is that many returning missionaries lose sight of this fact. Don't be one of them.

8

A Return on God's Investment

Jesus told the story of a master who had to leave on a trip. While he was gone, the master entrusted the care of his possessions to his servant. Unfortunately, the master was delayed on his trip, and the servant began to act up. When the master finally returned and saw what the servant was doing with his possessions, he had the servant punished. In concluding this parable, Jesus said, "From everyone who has been given much, much will be demanded; and from the one who has been entrusted with much, much more will be asked" (Luke 12:48).

When a person invests money in the stock market, in a building project, or in a trust fund—even in a savings account—that person expects to get a return on that investment. They anticipate that their investment will make a profit.

What has God given you as a result of your missions exposure and experience? What has He entrusted to you? Many of you will have stepped out and walked by faith. In the process, you have seen the reality of God, much like Peter did when he stepped out and walked on the water. You also have had the unique opportunity of seeing and experiencing firsthand things that others only read about in books and magazines, or see on television. You have lived in a foreign culture among people who think and act differently than you. As a result, you have changed; you are not the same person you were when you left for the mission field. After you return, what will be God's return on all that He has invested in you during your time on the mission field?

For the rest of your life, you will carry with you the sights, sounds, and impressions you experienced on the mission field. While there, you will also have developed an awareness of the physical, emotional, and spiritual needs of other missionaries, and of the people you were seeking to reach with the Gospel.

When you arrive home, you become a link between two unknowns in a very real sense: the people group among whom you served and who are unknown to your church congregation, and your church congregation, which is unknown to the people group. The one group has a desperate need; the other group has the means to help meet that need. And you can be a bridge between the two.

You have a unique perspective and a unique opportunity to bring to your church a greater level of awareness of needs on the mission field, particularly in the area where you served. By doing this, you can still have an impact on the mission field, even though you are at home.

The question that arises is, "How can I do this? How can I take the experiences of the mission field and see them multiplied for the kingdom of God? How can I transfer to others in my church what God has invested in me during my time away?"

Be an Advocate

The dictionary says that an advocate is one who "speaks on behalf of another, to plead for, to defend, to recommend publicly." As a returning missionary, you have the opportunity to become an advocate for the people group you have served among. You can speak to other Christians on their behalf. You can help Christians to see the desperate need these people have to hear the Gospel. You can inform others about people they know little or nothing about. You can rally people to pray for them, to give toward supporting other missionaries serving among them. You can even challenge other Christians to consider going on a short-term outreach to work among the people group.

You are the advocate for these people, and you must use every opportunity available to advance and articulate their needs. You are the champion of their cause in your local church and geographic area. Your work among this people group on the mission field does not stop when you get home; it expands! Following are some practical ways by which you can translate the theory of being an advocate into practice.

Be Informed

Continue to take an interest in the people group you worked among on the mission field. Keep abreast of the group's changing political and social position. The political and social situation of many developing nations is constantly shifting, so do your best to stay current.

It may be that you would like to return to work among this people group at some time in the future. If you are fluent in their language, practice using it so you won't lose your fluency, even if it means talking out loud to yourself. If you are not fluent in the language, you may want to take the time to learn the language properly.

It is also helpful to keep up your relationships with members of the people group you befriended while there. A letter is the easiest way to do this. If they are unable to read or write, you may want to record your message onto a cassette, then arrange for a missionary on the field to play it to the person, record their response, and send it back to you. This provides you with a good source of information on those individuals to whom you ministered, and on the people group in general.

The embassy of the nation where the people group is located is also a good source of updated information, as are public libraries.

With the more open immigration policies that many western nations have, it is quite possible that there is a community of people living in your nation or city who have emigrated from the particular ethnic or people group you were working among. If so, search them out, and befriend members of the community. Not only will you be updated about information relating to the people group, but you can continue ministering to those people. You can be their cross-cultural missionary. And you can take others from your church with you, introducing them to the people group and to cross-cultural missions.

Be an Intercessor

"We always thank God for all of you, mentioning you in our prayers. We continually remember before our God and Father your work produced by faith, your labor prompted by love, and your endurance inspired by hope in our Lord Jesus

Christ" (I Thessalonians 1:2-3).

Paul understood the value of prayer. While on the mission field, you probably felt the reassurance of knowing others were praying for you. It is such a morale-booster for a missionary to know there are people committed enough to pray on a regular basis. The work of the missionary and the work of the intercessor go hand in hand.

God is able to do amazing things when we pray. For years, Christians have prayed that God would tear down the gates of communism which have kept missionaries out of Eastern Europe and the Soviet Union. While godless Communist regimes persecuted Christians, and declared themselves to be atheist states, God patiently waited to set His plan in motion, borne on the prayers of intercessors. When the time was right, the walls of communism crumbled, and the gates swung open for missionaries to enter.

But that is only the beginning. Even though missionaries have entered the land, we must now "take the land" through the power of the Gospel. We must win the hearts and minds of the people to Christ. And that is an even bigger challenge than praying to see communism torn down. Now we must pray for the walls in each person's heart to be torn down so the Gospel might renew their lives. It is accomplished by missionaries, who actually share with the people, and by intercessors, who hold the situation up before God in prayer.

What about the people group among whom you served? You have the opportunity of rallying intercessors together to "stand in the gap" (Ezekiel 22:30). You have the privilege of joining forces with other missionaries by praying for them. This blesses them in the same way that you were blessed by knowing others were praying for you while you were on the mission field.

Be a Giver

While serving on the mission field, you were probably the recipient of other people's generosity, either through monthly support, one-time financial gifts, or other gifts such as goods and clothing from home. Once home, one of the best ways to keep your heart tied to the mission field is through financially supporting other missionaries.

Jesus tells us that where our treasure is our heart will be, too (Luke 12:34). So invest your finances and your heart back into missions.

You may not feel that you can make much of a contribution if you're returning home for further schooling, or if you can't land a well-paying job right away. But the amount is not as important as the heart from which it is given. Remember the widow's mite? Jesus told us that she was more generous than all the rich people who gave, because she had given out of her need, not her excess (Mark 12:44). The amount may have been small, but the heart of the widow was right in giving it.

Look for creative opportunities to give. In some cases, it may be more useful to the missionary you are supporting to send specific items that they have requested, or items you know they will need, rather than sending cash.

Don't forget that as an advocate, you should challenge other Christians to become financial supporters of the missionaries working among that people group.

Be Supportive

This is a much broader category than just sending a support check to a missionary at the end of the month. There are many other ways in which missionaries need support. You can probably think of many of these ways from your own experience. Missionaries need people back home to help with their financial matters, to send newspaper clippings and familiar food items, to copy and send out their newsletters, or hospitable people to stay with when they return home. Write to your friends who are still on the mission field, and ask in what practical ways you can be of assistance to them. Or better still, discuss it with them before you leave the mission field. Again, try to involve other Christians from your church in this, as well, so they can gain more exposure to missions and missionaries.

Be Part of a Missions Board

You have fresh insights and up-to-the-minute experience and enthusiasm to offer a missions board. Being on a board gives you an outlet for your experience and knowledge, as well as giving you insight into the area of sending and supporting missionaries within the local church context. Remember, though, that many churches have their own structure and requirements regarding mission boards, and it may not be possible for you to be a member of such a board in your church. However, you can pray for those who are on the board, that they would be granted wisdom in making their decisions. You can also offer to serve them in any way they may need help.

It is also possible that your church does not have a missions board. If that is the case, talk to the pastor about the possibility of forming one. Ask in humility, remembering that "love does not insist on its own way" (I Corinthians 13:4 RSV).

Perhaps your pastor is not open to the idea of a church-sanctioned missions board, but would allow you to form an informal group to pray for missionaries, and to conduct a group Bible study with a strong emphasis on missions.

In pursuing this, I recommend an excellent book, *Serving as Senders*, by Neal Pirolo.[3] Pirolo explores many of the ways in which a person at home can become a vital part of a missionary's support team. He also deals with how to offer moral, logistical, financial, prayer, communication, and re-entry support to missionaries. He also makes a strong theological argument regarding the need for "senders" as well as "goers." If you cannot become a part of your church's mission board, you can at least give a copy of this book to your pastor and to the members of the board.

Be a Recruiter

God may have called you home so you can be instrumental in sending ten more people to the mission field to take your place. In an earlier chapter, I mentioned that only five percent of those who acknowledge they had been called to the mission field ever make it there. What about the other ninety-five percent? For a few, outright disobedience and rebellion keep them from going. But I am convinced that many people do not make it because they simply do not know how to go about getting there. They have no missionary role model in their church to follow. They are unaware of the steps needing to be taken from the call to actually going to the mission field.

This is where you come in. You have experience as a returned missionary. You know the steps that must be followed, and you can communicate those steps to people who feel God is calling them to the mission field. You can mentor other Christians in how to become a missionary.

Pray that you might recognize those God has His hand upon, whom you can nurture to the point where they are ready to set out in faith for the mission field. Such nurturing may take the form of lending them good missions books, sharing your experiences with them, leading them in a Bible study that emphasizes the importance God places on missions, or just listening to and addressing any fears they may have.

You can have the privilege of playing a part in helping another Christian grow into the call God has placed upon his life.

Stay Linked with Your Mission Agency

Don't expect too much from the mission agency you served with. Everyone wishes their agency maintained both constant contact with them and an active interest in all they do. But in reality, that is seldom the case. The mission organization you leave will continue to grow and change. If the secretary leaves—the one who knew where to find your address and the kinds of things you would like to be kept informed about—she may fail to pass on the information to the new secretary. And since most mission organizations are under-staffed, things such as communicating with past workers—which should be a priority—get pushed down to a lower rung on the ladder of importance.

For these reasons, you need to take the initia-tive. Instead of waiting for the mission agency to communicate with you, you communicate with it. Remember, your mission agency is not an office, a name on a letterhead, a slogan, or even a cause; it

is people. If there are no people, there is no agency.
So communicating with your agency becomes a
matter of maintaining relationships. It is keeping
connections open with the people God called you
to labor with during your time on the mission field.

The apostle Paul was a master at keeping in
touch with those he had labored with. As a result,
much of the New Testament is a compilation of his
letters. When you write to those you served with,
follow the example of Paul's letters. Offer encouragement and a sympathetic ear to your former
co-workers. Many missionaries have no one with
whom they feel comfortable sharing deep hurts
and problems. As one who has been on the mission
field you are in the unique position of being outside the immediate situation while being able to
empathize with the person and understand what
he is going through.

Check to see if your mission organization has
an alumni group to keep people in touch with each
other and with what is happening in the agency
itself. If there is not one in your area, and there
are others in your vicinity who also served with the
agency, you may want to start an alumni group.

Doubtless your mission organization has a
magazine or some other publication that is produced periodically, so make sure you are on the
subscription list to receive it. In Youth With A
Mission, for example, most centers put out their
own newsletters. In addition, the organization produces a bimonthly video newsmagazine, which
features news and missions updates from around
the world. Also, YWAM Associates International
publishes an alumni magazine called "In Touch,"
and plans renewal camps for associates and their
friends. All these resources are useful in helping

those who have served in Youth With A Mission to stay in touch with the organization.

Investigate resources that your mission has for staying in touch...and stay in touch!

The City That Is to Come

"For here we do not have an enduring city, but we are looking for the city that is to come" (Hebrews 13:14). As you return home, this verse reminds that you are not returning to an enduring city. Your identity is not tied to your geographic location or your ethnic group. Your identity is in the city that is to come, and that is where you must place your focus.

God has made an investment in your life. He has sent you to the mission field, provided for you, and blessed you. As you return home, He is looking for a return on that investment. Are you going to settle back into your comfortable lifestyle and forget the lessons you learned on the field? Are you going to forget the physical and spiritual needs of the people to whom you strove to bring the Gospel? Are you going to compartmentalize your life and say, "that was then and this is now"?

Or are you going to allow the experiences of the mission field to change the way you live? Are you going to live the rest of your life focusing on the city that is to come? Are you going to be an advocate for the unreached peoples of the earth who desperately need to hear and experience the life-changing message of the Gospel?

What is God's return on His investment going to be? The choice is yours. For the sake of those who have not yet had the opportunity to hear the Gospel, I pray that you choose to apply your life to seeking the city that is to come.

Appendices

Appendices

Before You Go into Missions

A Checklist

The best re-entry preparation starts before you leave home. Following are nine things you can do prior to heading out into missions that will set the stage for your return.

- Tell as many people as possible, including family members, your pastor, home group, people in your church, co-workers, and friends, that you are going to the mission field. Explain what you will be doing there, your reasons for going, and how long you expect to be away.
- Let some of your friends know how much you would like to receive letters from them.
- Commit to write to these people on a regular basis, sharing news and photos of yourself and your mission. When you write to them, be honest and real. Don't overspiritualize things. Find the balance in your letters between "uppers"— those triumphal epistles of habitual success— and "downers"—the defeatist dispatches cataloging endless moans about hardships and lack of finances.
- Approach a few proven intercessors, asking them to pray for you and your mission while you are away. Choose people you can share your heart with, having no fear of disclosure. Then you can leave with absolute confidence

that you have a team of committed people who
are frequently lifting you and your ministry up
to the throne of God.

- Ensure that you are properly sent out. If it is
  not possible to be publicly sent out. If it is not
  possible to be publicly prayed for in your
  church before you leave, ask your pastor and
  his staff to commend you in prayer at a time
  convenient for them.
- Be commissioned by your home fellowship
  group, whose members will probably be your
  closest church contacts while you are away.
  Also, if your family members are Christians,
  have them gather around to pray for you and
  send you off. If your family members are not believers, simply ask them to let you go with their
  blessing.
- Ask a Sunday school class to adopt you, encouraging them to pray for you, your ministry, and
  the needs of the culture in which you will be
  serving. Challenge the class to tithe from their
  allowance to help support a specific project on
  the mission field. Regularly send them postcards and photographs; don't send the tourist
  type, but ones that portray the real conditions
  and needs on the mission field.
- Commit to pray regularly for your family,
  church, friends, city, and country. Then do it.
- Take care of your financial affairs. Credit spending is learned early in life, and can easily en-
  snare the unwary. If necessary, sell what you
  have, and take any other steps needed to become as debt-free as possible. And make sure
  you leave someone with power of attorney over
  your financial affairs. Should something happen while you are away, or your return is delayed, you will be glad you gave someone that
  authority.

Debriefing
in a Group Context

In Chapter One, we spoke about the importance of bringing closure to our time on the mission field through debriefing. Short-term mission teams are an important reality today, either on a summer outreach or as part of a missionary or discipleship training program. Here's how to undertake a time of debriefing in this group context. While debriefing is vitally important to rounding out a person's experience on the mission field, it is often overlooked.

Debriefing in a group context is best accomplished with six or more people who have a shared experience. But if there are fewer, don't let that stop you.

Ideally, the leader of the group or team should act as the facilitator, making sure sufficient time is set aside before the team disbands to complete this process. For two people to work through the process as a pair and reap the maximum benefit, it should take about a day. This time should be adjusted proportionally if you intend to complete step three, which is advised. And don't forget Step Four. It is important, even if you skip Step Three.

Step One: Try to set aside at least three hours by yourself: first mediate on Philippians 4:8-9, then reflect back over your missions experience, jotting down:

- Any insights you have learned about yourself and about missions.
- What you intend to do with what you have learned, i.e., your goals.
- Any obstacles that might keep you from achieving your goals (e.g., fears, uncertainties, lack of strategy).

- Your plan for achieving your goals and for overcoming any obstacles you may have identified.

Write down your findings as concisely as possible. A
notebook, your diary/journal, and your Bible are essential
for this step.

Step Two: Pair off, preferably with someone you don't
know too well--this helps both of you to be more objective.
Share with the person what you have noted in Step One.
Receive feedback about these observations from your partner. Have your partner pray for you. Then reverse the
process by having your partner share the four points with
you, and so on.

Step Three: If there is enough time and the group is big
enough, put three pairs of people together, and repeat all
you did in Step Two in this larger group. Then everyone
should come together, and a spokesperson from each group
should take fifteen minutes to summarize their group's
feelings about the missions experience.

Step Four: Each person will then take a sheet of paper
and write himself a letter based upon his findings from the
reflection time, adding any helpful feedback from the
others. Place the letter in an envelope, seal it, and address
it to your permanent address. The leader should collect the
letters and arrange to mail them out in about five months'
time. When the letter arrives, it will serve as a good checkup
on your progress in re-entry and in applying the insights
and lessons learned on the mission field to your life at
home.

If you follow this simple plan for debriefing, it will help
you receive the maximum in your life for the time spent on
the mission field. Too many people go into missions, then
return home without ever adequately reflecting upon their
experiences, individually or corporately, and without deter-
mining what they have learned and how they are going to
integrate that learning into their lives once they arrive
home.

(Thanks to Dr. Rachel Kass, psychologist and short-
term missionary, for these insights.)

Short-term Missions and the Local Church

by Floyd McClung, Jr.

God is using short-term mission experiences to deepen the commitment to world evangelization in the hearts of young and old alike. But difficulties arise if the church and the mission organization do not cooperate to see God's maximum blessing for the church, the mission, and the individual.

While serving in another culture, the short-term volunteers can see firsthand some of the lostness of the world, as well as some of the hurts and needs that exist in other cultures. As a result, they return home with a new sense of dedication to God, and a new fire burning in their hearts to make their lives count for Him.

Some short-term workers feel called to go on to a career of missionary service. Others find it obvious that what they thought was a missionary call was human enthusiasm. Still others become significantly involved in the ongoing mission thrust of the church, where God can use their experience as a spark to light others with a commitment to world evangelism.

Unfortunately, some short-term workers do not remain actively committed to missions for the local church. Why? Their enthusiasm for missions is dulled by the pressures they face when they return home. They don't integrate the blessings of the short-term experience into service in the church.

How can the local church and the missionary organization encourage these individuals to stay vitally involved in world evangelization? And how can they be encouraged and challenged for effective service in the local church when they return?

The following suggestions are made to help initiate positive policies in the church to guide those who want to be involved in short-term missions. These policies should not be used to control people or keep them back from service, but to give them guidelines and let them understand what the local church expects from them if they are going to be sent out with the blessing of the church. In this way, people can understand clearly what is required of them, and will be better prepared for their return after the short-term experience.

Obviously the burden is not entirely on the local church to make the short-term experience meaningful. It is a matter of mutual accountability between the church and the mission agency to see God's full blessing realized in the lives of all those involved. Let's work together to make the short-term experience for the person going out from the church all that God wants it to be.

Screening and Stewardship

The Church's Mission Policies

Each church should develop its own mission policies. This would include developing a manual or paper that outlines the policies and who is responsible (e.g. the Pastor of Missions or the Missions Committee) to implement the policies. In other words, if someone wants to go out in short-term service, the pastor can refer him to either the Missions Committee or the Pastor of Missions.

The policies should outline the qualifications the short-termer must meet, the church's philosophy of missions, and the application process for those to be sent out with the church's blessing. In this way, the burden is taken off the pastor or the leadership of the church to make individual decisions as to whether or not people can be involved.

For example, if someone wants to be involved in a short-term missions project, but has not been faithful in attendance in the church, has never offered to help in teaching Sunday school, or has not been available to be practical responsibilities when asked, it can be pointed out that the policy of the church states that the church will back only those who are active and consistent in attendance and service. The standards should not be too strict, or people will never be able to attain them, but they should involve some sacrifice. This gives the church a chance to screen those they send out.

Perhaps the reason some people don't integrate successfully back into the local church is because they were immature when they went out. If the church takes more responsibility for screening those who go out, it is more likely that when people come back from a short-term experience, they will feel more accountability to the local church.

Stewards of the Experience

Every person involved in short-term missions should be encouraged to view himself as a steward of his short-term experience. These experiences are not only for personal edification, career guidance, or a one-time contribution to missions, but are also given to individuals by God to be used for the good of the local church.

Short-term workers need to build what they have learned into the lives of others, and help the local church move forward in missions. This means the short-term workers should be given orientation and instruction before they are selected and sent out by the local church. Those not presently involved in the life of the church, or not willing to be multipliers of the vision upon their return, are not the best candidates for the church's investment. Short-term workers should view themselves as stewards of their experiences for the good of the entire Body.

Who Pays for It?

The church's involvement financially for those going out in short-term experiences will obviously vary from church to church. This depends on the size of the church, the maturity of the person, how long he has been actively involved in the church, and how many short-termers may be going out at any one time.

A basic rule-of-thumb that many churches have found to work well is to ask those who are going to summer programs, Bible school, or other training programs, to be responsible to raise their own finances. (Obviously, the church may wish to encourage its members to give to those going out in these situations, but they would still recognize the responsibility of those going to pay their own way.) The church can make it clear that its commitment is to help raise support for those doing long-term missions, or one- and two-year short-term commitments. In this way, the church is making financial investments in those who have shown initiative and responsibility, and have proven themselves in the church and in short-term endeavors.

Orientation and Preparation

Get Ready

It is helpful for the local church to provide orientation for those going out in short-term experiences. This should include the church's view of missions, what the church expects of the people while they are involved (e.g., reports, letters) and the adjustments the short-termer should expect as they go into a new situation or culture. It is helpful for the local church to have those who have had missionary experience share with potential candidates what they will experience when they leave home and go to another nation. Materials may be available from the mission agency to help with the task.

Be Accountable

One pastor I know reminds young people that when they go out, their accountability is to the authority of the local church, and he does not want them making any long-term decisions until they report back to the church. Upon the missionary's return, he will meet with the Missions Pastor or Missions Committee and review how beneficial his experience was, how well he did when he was in the mission experience, and how well he integrates back into the local church. This kind of oversight, preparation, and orientation produces not only a better prepared candidate, but also a greater level of accountability in people's lives to the Lord and to the local church.

The Re-Entry Process

Know Before You Go

It is the responsibility of both the mission agency and the local church to prepare its volunteers for the re-entry process into the local church. Short-term workers need to be adequately debriefed, and helped to process their experiences upon their return. It is the responsibility of the mission to remind the short-term workers that they should not compare their experience on the short-term situation (where they have experienced many hours of prayer, evangelism, relationship building, worship, etc.) with the life of the local church.

There are two different structures involved: the missions structure and the local church structure. God raised up each for different purposes. It's too easy for people to compare the mission experience with the life of the local church, and draw negative conclusions. People are to be reminded of God's purpose for the local church. It provides the nurture and resources for 95 percent of God's people! This means that those involved in 9 a.m. to 5 p.m. jobs, who are salt and light in the world, are called by God to be there.

It is important to remind the short-termer (and to actively teach and practice) that the local church is also a mission structure, called to support those who have been led by God to serv e Him as His ambassadors in the work world. Sometimes it is much easier to be involved in foreign missions than it is to be involved in the business world, the factory, or the local school. Christians need to be reminded of the vital role the local church plays in world missions.

Talk It Out

When short-term workers return to the local church, they must be able to discuss what they saw God do; what things changed their attitudes, perspectives, and priorities;

and what they learned about their gifts and abilities. These subjects need to be dealt with lovingly and carefully with others who can help the short-term workers evaluate and respond to their findings.

Short-term workers need people from their local church who will listen reflectively over a period of months as the returned missionaries integrate their new experiences into their home culture. We suggest that somebody from the local church met weekly with those who have been involved in short-term missions. The prayer, counseling, and reflection will help them successfully integrate back into the life of the church. They need those who will understand what they are feeling, and encourage them in the learning process. They need those who will direct them in practical ways to be catalysts for missions in the church. Meeting and sharing with others who represent the leadership of the church, and who have a positive view toward the church and missions, can be extremely useful in helping people reintegrate into the local church.

There will be adjustments. It is natural to come back excited and anxious to share with others. Encourage their enthusiasm, but also be there to help when the zeal dies down and they return to school or work. This letdown can be accompanied by criticism and comparisons, but if they are challenged and guided as they work through these adjustments, tremendous growth can take place. We recommend that local churches send elders or mature members on short-term outreaches so they understand firsthand the experience of their members.

Get Involved

It is also important for the local church to have programs that challenge the young people and other short-term workers for constructive service once they come back to the local church. When the short-term workers come back fired up, but find no opportunity for service, they can become disillusioned and disappointed.

One church had an evangelism program every September for all those who came out of short-term summer experiences. This puts the responsibility back on the short-term worker not to be critical of the local church, but to "put their money where their mouth is." It also puts responsibility on the church to lead by example.

Get Feedback

Short-term workers also need positive, objective feedback in writing about their experiences. A simple form would be shown to them before their outreach, and completed after their return. This can be useful in helping them evaluate their growth and understand how the church sees them. This will show the short-term workers how others see their strengths and weaknesses, and help direct them to areas needing work in preparation for future ministry.

If the local church also requests an evaluation from the mission on how the worker did, it can be helpful in this feedback process. This long-range re-entry process is the responsibility of both the local church and the mission agency. The mission organization obviously has a great responsibility in this process, but because people come out of the local church, the church must take primary responsibility for the re-entry process.

When short-term missionaries are screened, receive orientation, understand their stewardship responsibilities, and have an established re-entry process, the fires that have been lit in their lifes can continue to burn. Some practical steps can be taken to keep those first burning in the hearts of those who feel called.

- They should share the burden on their heart with the leadership of the church, and they should be encouraged to develop it. Opportunity should be given to do this on a regular basis so the church is not surprised when they hear of it in a letter from Mexico or Europe! Aspiring missionaries and enthusiastic short-termers should be told that the church wants to encourage them, but doesn't want surprises. As the church takes initiative, it has maximum opportunity to counsel and influence them in their decisions and preparations.

- They should read missionary biographies that will help inspire them to believe that God can use them.
- They should be encouraged to faithful service in the local church.
- The church should challenge them to be involved in mission outreaches in the local area, in nearby cities, states, and in other countries to keep them actively involved in witnessing and sharing their faith.
- They should be encouraged to stay out of debt.
- They should be counseled to marry someone who has a similar calling.
- They should get on the mailing list of several mission agencies to keep current on prayer information.
- They should be encouraged to intercede regularly for the lost and for the nations of the world. It would be helpful to read P.J. Johnstone's book, *Operation World,* and to use Youth With A Mission's *Personal Prayer Diary* (which serves as a practical diary for appointments and addresses, lists all the nations of the world for prayer, and gives helpful information about quiet times, Bible meditation, and intercession).
- They should write to various mission agencies to familiarize themselves with the different programs, philosophies, and approaches to missions so that they can pray intelligently about which one they should be involved in.

Notes

1--Thanks to Kelly O'Donnell (PsyD) and Michele O'Donnell (PsyD) for preparing these self-assessment points.

2--*What is a Family?*, Edith Schaeffer, Hodder & Stoughton, 1975.

3--*Serving As Senders*, Neal Pirolo, Emmaus Road International, 7150 Tanner Court, San Diego CA 92111.

Notes

Recommended Reading

- *Is That Really You, God?*, by Loren Cunningham ($7.99 US)
  See how an ordinary man who was determined to hear God and obey Him, became the founder of an extraordinary missionary organization. This book is a practical guide to hearing the voice of God.

- *Daring to Live on the Edge*, by Loren Cunningham ($7.99 US)
  A compelling, fresh look at faith and finances; trust and provision by one of America's premier missions statesmen. This book will challenge and equip those who want to obey God's call to step out in faith, but wonder where the money will come from.

- *Stepping Out*, compiled by Hawthorne, Moy, and Krekel ($8.99 US)
  This book is a great tool to motivate, clarify expectations, inform of opinions, shape attitudes, and prepare you for adjusting to new cultures and working conditions. *Stepping Out* is a powerful resource for those who are preparing for short-term mission involvement or work in any capacity related to training and placement for support of missions.

- *Friend Raising*, by Betty Barnett ($8.99 US)
  Friend Raising brings together God's plan for biblical missions support with principles proven in the field. This book is a strong dose of common sense, mixed with that rare spice, respect for the donor, and liberally garnished with the conviction that God supplies needs through mutually satisfying relationships. In a world overwhelmed with fund raising hype and gimmicks, Betty Barnett's book is a refreshing biblical alternative.

- *Spiritual Warfare for Every Christian*, by Dean Sherman ($9.99 US)
  Spiritual warfare is everyone's responsibility! And it is more than rebuking demons. Dean delivers a no-nonsense, balanced, and practical approach to this dynamic and important area of Christian living.
  Spiritual Warfare is also available on 12 cassettes for $39.99 US or 12-1 hour videos for $120.00 US

- *Personal Prayer Diary/Daily Planner,* ($14.99 US)
  Join tens of thousands of believers worldwide to pray for the
  unreached peoples of the world. This diary/planner is a unique
  tool that will maximize your global prayer efforts. Included in
  the diary is: weekly, monthly, and yearly at-a-glance sections,
  Bible reading guide, quiet time journal, world maps, daily
  prayer points, and much more. Get organized and increase your
  daily prayer time effectiveness.

- *Tracking Your Walk, (Youth Journal and Prayer Diary)*
  ($12.99 US)
  This exciting tool is designed for ages 9 and older with 3 key
  areas in mind: Introducing the younger Christian to the quiet
  time/journaling discipline, developing consistent Bible reading
  and memorization habits, and prayer for the nations and peoples of the world. Undated, this journal can be started at any
  time.

- *Mandate for Mercy,* by Don Stephens ($8.99 US)
  This book is a powerful and compassionate "call to arms" for
  Christians everywhere. This compelling teaching and collection
  of stories vividly demonstrates that individuals, working
  together for God's glory, can and do make a lasting impact on
  this hurting, suffering world in which we live. This book is
  wonderfully enhanced with unforgettable stories from the
  annals of the "Mercy Ships" worldwide ministry voyages.

- *The "GO" Manual,* ($2.99 US)
  Discover thousands of short or long-term missions opportunities
  available with *Youth With A Mission* world-wide. This annually
  updated manual contains hundreds of contact addresses and
  phone numbers allowing you to pursue missions and training
  opportunities in over 100 nations of the world.

International Adventures
(Look for ongoing new releases in the "International Adventures" series)

- *Dayuma: Life Under Waorani Spears,* by Ethel Emily Wallis ($8.99 US)
  Jim Elliot, Nate Saint, Pete Fleming, Roger Youderian, and Ed McCully chose to lay down their lives on a sandy beach in Ecuador. Their lives and sacrifice come full circle in the breathtaking true story of Dayuma. This book is the unforgettable story of one girl's odyssey into the unknown. Her encounter with Christ ultimately changed her life and forever altered the destiny of her people.

- *Adventures in Naked Faith,* by Ross Tooley ($8.99 US)
  As an eighteen year old, Ross Tooley brought to the mission field a heart of zeal and compassion…and an untested faith. The tests began immediately. During three decades of ministry that led him from his New Zealand home to the Philippines and around the world, Ross uncovered and lived out principles to building a reliable faith. This book is sure to challenge you to seek God for your path in life, confident that whom God calls He also prepares and provides for.

- *The Man with the Bird On His Head,* by John Rush & Abbe Anderson ($8.99 US)
  Cargo cult villagers march in formation at the base of a rumbling fiery volcano. Their ancient prophecies predict the return of a mysterious messenger. Are these prophecies about to come true? Sail with the crew of a medical mission ship into the middle of the hopes and history of this unreached Pacific people group.

- *Praying Through the 100 Gateway Cities of the 10/40 Window,* by Wagner/Peters/Wilson ($8.99 US)
  Tens of thousands of Christians worldwide have used this book to pray for the major unreached cities of the 10/40 window. Join with the multitudes in prayer that the gospel would go forth to those who have not yet heard.

- **Strongholds of the 10/40 Window,** by George Otis, Jr. ($12.99 US)
  The 10/40 window is the primary spiritual frontier for the gospel in the world today. The Sentinel Group produced this manual as a handbook for those who are serious about the role of prayer as a tool in global evangelism.

- **The Unreached Peoples,** by Johnstone, Hanna, Smith ($8.99 US)
  This book is the follow-up to *Praying Through the 100 Gateway Cities of the 10/40 Window. The Unreached Peoples* is an invaluable prayer guide to join with thousands of believers worldwide to pray for specific people groups who have yet to hear the gospel.